King Sejong the Great

Prepared by
Diamond Sutra Recitation Group

Acknowledgment for Copyright Release

The following organization and individuals have graciously released their copyrights:

Bae, Kichan

Jeon, Sang-woon

Kim, Ho

Pak, Song-rae

King Sejong Memorial Society

King Sejong the Great:

The Everlasting Light of Korea

Prepared by
Diamond Sutra Recitation Group

ISBN: 0-9779613-6-2

Printed in Korea

For all inquiries contact **kingsejong@mail.com**

King Sejong the Great

The Everlasting Light of Korea

Korean Spirit and Culture Website

Admiral Yi Sun-sin

King Sejong the Great

Coming soon...

Sim Chong and Other Stories

Sin Saimdang

Queen Sondok

General Ulchimundok

Master Wonhyo

www.koreanhero.net

www.koreanpatriot.net

For all inquiries contact kingsejong@mail.com

King Sejong the Great

Contents

Appendix

The Sillok: the Royal Annals of Choson Dynasty

The History of the Rain Gauge

Bibliography

I. General Remarks

"If the people prosper, how can the king not prosper with them?
And if the people do not prosper, how may the king prosper without them?"
King Sejong, 4th Ruler of Choson Korea

The Chinese of the early 15th century referred to their king as 'Son of the Heavens', while isolationist Japan gave the title 'Ruler of the Heavens' to its emperor. At a time when the monarchs of neighbouring states were glorifying their offices with divine-like honours, King Sejong of Korea established the notion of the 'People of the Heavens'. Sejong, who revered each and every one of his people as being of Heavenly origin and served them as such, believed that the duty of a king was no more than to look after the people of a noble, heavenly race.

Sejong's care and attention extended to every member of his kingdom. Female servants in government office, for example, were given thirty days of leave prior to giving birth, and a further 100 days of leave afterwards, while their husbands were granted thirty days of paternity leave. He also considered the rights of prisoners, frequently inquiring after the temperatures at which the prisons were being kept, and ensuring that they were kept clean and maintained properly. The 'People of the Heavens', in King Sejong's view, were not simply the people of Korea. Even foreign peoples, such as the tribes of Jurchens, then considered by Korea and China as barbarians, were, as he believed, no less worthy of his respect. His views are all the more remarkable, if we consider that this was an age in which men were classed by common perception as either civilized or barbaric.

He did not regard the people simply as objects of his care and governance, but believed that they possessed a limitless potential to transform, realize, and awaken themselves to a higher cultural and spiritual level. To help them achieve this, as he thought, was the real duty of kings and officials. The great efforts he devoted to developing the new alphabet *Hangul* and to advance printing technology for the publication of books on many and various subjects were all made to achieve this one end of helping the heavenly race of mankind educate and improve itself.

"To share in the joys of living with Heaven's People" was the goal of King Sejong, and he never rested for a moment in his pursuit of it. When his people starved, he starved with them and prepared himself for death, offering up prayers to Heaven. Even when his eyesight became seriously impaired and his health was in a grave condition, he sacrificed everything he had for his people. He fortified the nation's defences by strengthening the army and improving its standards of weaponry. He also revolutionized the sciences, particularly those of agriculture, medicine and astronomy. A scientific dictionary, published in Japan in 1983, recorded that twenty-nine of the world's scientific achievements in the early 15th century were made in Korea, five in China, none in Japan, and twenty-six in the rest of the world. In step with scientific progress, literature and the arts also flourished, and the people's standard of living greatly rose substantially.

In politics, King Sejong's reign was characterized by democratic discussion and constructive partnerships, founded upon mutual respect and tolerance. *Kyong-yon*, a formal occasion for reading and debate between the king and his courtiers, took place at least once a week during Sejong's reign, 1,898 times in total. Through discussions of this kind, the king was able to identify and resolve issues of national importance, and took care to ensure that every man's voice would be heard, regardless of his social position. An extract from the *Sillok*, an official shorthand record of the king's affairs, describes the courtiers' staunch opposition to Sejong's introduction of *Hangul* and his proposal to build a Buddhist temple in the grounds of the Royal Palace (the state religion of Korea was at that time Confucianism, and the King's practice of Buddhism was viewed with disapproval by certain members of the court). If we read Sejong's reply to their objections, it seems hard to believe that it is the speech of a dynastic autocrat of the fifteenth century. By means of judicious policies, improvements and reforms, the benevolent King Sejong led his country into a golden age.

There have been many rulers in the five thousand years of Korea's history, but Sejong is the only king to have been given the title 'Great' by the people of Korea, who even today remember his name and great wisdom with gratitude and respect.

II. The Historical Context

Sejong was born on the 15th of May, 1397 (April 10th by the lunar calendar) in the Chunsu district of the country's capital Hanyang (now Seoul), and given the birth name of To. He was the third son of Queen Wonkyong and King Taejong, himself the third in the line of the Choson kings. At the age of 12, he became a prince and was given the name of Chungnyong. At 16 he assumed the title of Grand Prince, and was inaugurated Crown Prince in June 1418, in place of his older brother Yangnyong. In August of the same year, he ascended to the throne as the fourth king of Choson Korea. His reign spanned more than 32 years, and he left many legacies behind him, such as *Hangul*. He died in April, 1450, at the age of 54, and his royal tomb is enshrined at the town of Nungsu, in Kyonggi Province.

Towards the close of the 14th century, the Choson dynasty was in the process of replacing the old dynasty of Koryo, and the country was undergoing a period of turbulent transition. The final years of Koryo (A.D. 918-1392) had been a particularly difficult time for the people. Amid the corruption of the ruling classes, the military had rebelled and foreign invasions had continued. The land tax system had also fallen into disorder, and looting by Japanese pirates was intensifying. Finally, General Yi Song-gye emerged as the central figure in the confused array of conflicting political factions, thanks to a series of splendid victories over the Hong-gun, the Jurchens, and the Japanese. In 1388, he disobeyed an order to conquer the town of Liao-tung, and instead marched his army back from Wihwa to seize power. He then ascended to the throne on July 16, 1392 as King Taejo, so establishing a new dynasty called *Choson*.

The shift from Koryo to Choson was more than a change of ruling family. It was a highly momentous event, and its reverberations were felt in every aspect of Korean life, from politics and economics, to government ideology and social customs. As the old forces of aristocracy declined and scholarly bureaucrats gained power, Neo-Confucianism, originally introduced during the late Koryo period, was adopted as the official creed of the Choson socio-political order, and made its way into the heart of its society. The resulting situation was quite different from the one which had prevailed during the Koryo period, when Confucianism and Buddhism had co-existed without quarrel or conflict. Reforms in the land tax system were also made by the new regime, and as a result the number and status of independent farmers increased, with many rising to join the middle-classes.

When Sejong was crowned in 1418, it had been 28 years since the founding of the new dynasty. While much of the public unrest and political confusion had by now calmed, thanks to the efforts of previous rulers, it was nevertheless a crucial period for Choson, and one on which the success of the new dynasty and Korea's new national identity would depend. Governing with compassion and wisdom, Sejong laid the foundations of a royal household that would endure for another 500 years, leading Korea into an extraordinary era of cultural and scientific progress, unmatched by any other nation of the day. The golden age enjoyed by Korea during the 15th century is an example of how, in the words of the proverb, an era produces a leader, and the leader leads it forward.

Kyonghi Hall at Kyongbok Palace

III. The Character and Spirit of King Sejong

Sejong firmly believed that it was the duty and mission of a king to serve his country as well as he possibly could, and to sacrifice himself for the sake of its people. The people's happiness was the sole standard against which he measured his success as ruler. This chapter contains various extracts from the *Sillok*, or Annals of the Choson Dynasty, giving examples of Sejong's words and behaviour, and an insight into his character and spirit.

Love for the People

5 February, 3rd year of Sejong's Reign

By the Royal Order,

"The continuous flooding and drought of recent times have led to successive years of bad harvests. This last year has been particularly severe, and the lives of the people have become wretched. The Governor and the Chief Administrator of each province must provide relief for all, giving priority to the sick and handicapped. In due course, an official from the central government will tour and inspect the various districts. If it is discovered that there is one person who has died from starvation in the residential district of any province, the official responsible for that province will be convicted of felony."

3 July, 5th year

The King said,

"The common people are the foundation of any country. It is only when this foundation is strong that a country may be stable and prosperous."

20 June, 7th year

"The courtiers and officials will keep in mind the hardships of the people, and endeavour to point out every one of my faults, as well as errors and oversights in my ordinances and commands, so that I may fear the Heavens and have the utmost regard for the wellbeing of the people."

1 July, 7th year

The King said,

"The drought is too severe. There has been a shower, but it has merely filled the air with fog and dust. As this climate is abnormal, I will go out today to learn how the rice farmers have fared."

Whenever the King saw a rice field in poor condition, he would stop his horse and ask the farmer for the reason. When he returned later without having taken his midday meal, having thoroughly examined the fields outside the West Gate, he said to the courtiers,

"I was informed that the rice farming this year had been reasonably good, but when I saw the fields today, it brought tears to my eyes. How dry are Yongsoyok and Hongjewon, the areas I viewed today, compared to the rest of the country?"

28 July, 7th year

For the past ten days, since the 18th of the month, the King has stayed awake until dawn out of concern for the drought. He has become ill as a result, but has forbidden the announcement of his illness to the public.

23 February, 10th year

To the inspectors who were leaving to investigate reports of starvation in their provinces, the King said,

"Go in person to the hamlets hidden in the hills and the mountains, and if you come across a person in hunger, give him rice, beans, salt and soy sauce, and save his life. If a local governor has hidden anyone who has died or suffered from malnutrition, you must punish him according to the disciplinary laws. If his position is equal to or higher than 3 *pum*[1], you must first inform the Central Government. If his position is equal to or less than 4 *pum*, you may judge his offence there and then. If the need for relief is urgent, open the storehouses yourselves and give the people relief. "

18 December, 12th year

The King inquired about the state of harvest in each province, and discussed the assessment of land for taxation to be carried out that year by the officials.

Sin Sang of the Ministry of Rites said, "This year, the inspections have

---

[1] All government officials both civil and military were given ranks from 1 *pum* to 9 *pum*, with 1 *pum* being the highest level. Each *pum* was divided into two ranks: they were thus divided into 18 ranks all together.

been carried out on too lenient a basis."

To this the King replied, "I have heard that the people of Kyonggi are pleased that the inspections were lenient."

Sin Sang began to offer further arguments against the leniency of the inspection.

The King said to him, "It is not unjust that the inspection has been favourable to the public. If the people are satisfied, that is enough."

29 September, 14th year

When his horse ate a handful of rice from a farmer's store, the King said, "The farmer has taken great troubles to farm this rice, and since my horse has eaten it, he should receive what would have been due to him." He then ordered that the farmer be given a sack of rice in recompense.

21 June, 18th year

Another ordinance to the Ministry of Finance:

"The drought this year has again been more severe than usual. I am troubled for fear that the crops have been damaged and will not produce a good harvest.

The three Provinces of Chungchong, Kyongsang and Cholla must review their tributes to the Central Government, and declare which items should qualify for exemption, either on the basis that they are difficult to transport or that they are not essential to the State."

Another ordinance to the Ministry of Finance:

"Since the drought has been particularly severe in Chungchong Province, do not collect the barley grain, but let it be used as seed for next year's harvest."

25 July, 26th year

The King said,

"May the people work diligently, revere their parents, bring up their offspring wisely, and live long, so that the foundation of the country will be strong, every household plentiful, and every person affluent. May courtesy and humility arise in all men, so that we may dwell in lasting harmony and peace, gather in good harvests, and reap the joys of blessed and prosperous times. "

15 November, 31st year

The King said to Yi Kye-jon,

"In the Year of the Serpent [the 7th Year of the King's Reign, and a year of great drought], my illness became so grave and my chances of survival so small that a coffin was prepared for me by those outside the palace."

Filial Duty

When Sejong's father Taejong became ill, Sejong brought food and medicine to him in person, and when his condition worsened, Sejong stayed at his side throughout the night without taking any rest. When he learned of the death of his mother, Queen Wonkyong, he cast aside his wooden seat and lay upon a straw mat on the ground, lamenting in the rain both day and night.

According to Korean tradition, bereaved sons and daughters would mourn the death of a parent by wearing funeral garments, following a simple vegetarian diet, and leading a life of abstinence. During the mourning period for his parents, Sejong neglected his body to such an extent that the people grew very worried for his health.

10 February, 3rd year

Taejong passed away at the New Palace.

Since King Sejong would not eat, the government and the Six Ministries asked for permission to bring him porridge, but none was granted.

11 May, 4th year

Yun Sajong and Pyon Kaeryang said,

"Your Majesty has not eaten since he began to mourn the late king, and we are afraid that your body will be seriously harmed."

The King replied, "Yesterday the government and the Six Ministries submitted their pleas, and since you have pleaded again today, I will eat tonight."

After the evening ceremony, the ministers of government and the Six Ministries all came before him weeping, and declared,

"Ever since the late King's illness became critical, Your Majesty has not eaten. Remembering the warning of the sage, 'One should not harm one's life for the sake of the dead', restrain your sorrow and eat, so that your great piety may become whole."

In obedience to their request, the King accepted a bowl of thin porridge, but ate no more than once a day.

21 September, 4th year

Yi Chik, in company with others, said to the King,

"Even after the *cholgok* (a memorial service held in the third month after burial), your Majesty still eats only vegetables. Everyone is astonished at the sight of your haggard looks and dark complexion. Since you have eaten no meat for a long time, we are worried that Your Majesty may fall ill."

The King replied,

"Would it be seemly to dine on meat while I am in mourning? You are concerned that I may fall ill since I am not used to a diet of vegetables, but I am not ill now and have not offended against propriety in any way. Monks eat only vegetables, and yet some of them gain weight. How is it that only I cannot dine on vegetables? Do not speak of this again."

Respect for the Elderly

Worried that the senior courtiers might suffer from the summer heat, King Sejong searched for cool buildings in the palace grounds where they could work in comfort. He also invited the elderly to a banquet in their honour at the government offices in each of the Provinces, including the Royal Palace. It was the first time in Korean history that a king had invited the elderly to the Palace and dined with them in person.

17 August, 14th year

The Royal Secretariat said to His Majesty,

"Sire, do not invite the elderly of lowly origin to the banquet."

The King responded,

"I hold these banquets to honor the dignity of old age, not to measure rank and status. Therefore, permit entrance even to the lowest of the low, excluding only those bearing the mark of *chaja* (a tattoo on the face or the forearm, and the symbol of a convicted criminal)."

27 August, 14th year,

The King went out to the Kun-jong Hall to hold a dinner party for elderly men aged 80 or above. When several of them came out to the courtyard to bow before him, he ordered An Sung-son to stop them. The guests were divided between the East and the West side of the Palace, and the King ordered their sons, sons-in-law, nephews and other relatives help them to their seats.

At the end of the banquet, when all the guests had returned to the *pae-wi* (the place of bowing before the King), the King again ordered them to be prevented from bowing to him.

The King declared to the Secretaries,

"The weather today was clear and fine, and the banquet was successful, so I am pleased. We shall do as we did today when we receive the aged women at the banquet tomorrow."

3 August, 15th year

The King proceeded to the Kun-jong Hall for the feast. Again, he ordered that the elderly should not bow down before him, and when they came up in turn, he stood up to receive each guest. Towards the end of the banquet, some of the aged guests left singing and holding on to each other, happily intoxicated. During the banquet, Yi Kwi-ryong said, "This year I am 88, and of all the Kings I have lived under, none has treated the elderly with such respect as you have done today. Your Majesty held a banquet for us last year and fed us well, and now you have again given us a great feast, even standing up to receive old men like us when we approach your seat.

Although I may long consider how to repay your gracious acts, there is little I can do. I can only offer up prayers for your health and long life."

The King replied, "Your appearance was lean and thin last year, but this year you are full of lustre and health. I am very pleased."

28 August, 15th Year

An official letter to the Governor of the Provinces:

"In recognition of the fact that respect for the elderly is of great importance to a nation, I held a banquet in their honour for the first time in the Year of Imja [the 14th year of Sejong's reign]. However, I have heard that when local magistrates receive the elderly, they do not welcome them with kindness, and even when they do so, the selection of dishes they offer is so plain and meagre that their respect seems far less than it should be. Hereafter, any magistrate who does not perform this office wholeheartedly will be put on trial. Even the Governor of a Province will not escape culpability if he transgresses this command."

Fatherly Devotion

When his eldest daughter, Princess Chongso died unexpectedly in April 1424, Sejong's grief was beyond words. It is said that the king held on to the body of the princess and would not be parted from it, and that consequently the funeral preparations were delayed. The sudden loss of the twelve-year old princess so distressed him that he composed a memorial address to comfort the soul of his daughter.

How short or how long our lives will be has been ordained by fate and is unchangeable; but nothing can sever the bond of heart and mind which exists between a father and his daughter. Yours is a pitiful fate indeed. In your lifetime, from the days of tender youth, your conduct was calm and ordered, and your character refined and elegant. When we were walking together, your attitude towards your parents and siblings was full of warmth and sincere love. Though young, you were worthy of the respect which is due to age, and as my affections leaned towards you, my love and attachment grew all the more profound. I would often imagine your wedding in the future, and trusted that you would lead a life of happiness and comfort. Who could have foreseen that a mild illness would bring about this tragedy, and you be left with no more days to live? Evidently I did not have you cared for properly. Your soft voice and lovely appearance are still clear before my eyes, but as for your gracious, guiltless soul, where has it gone? I beat upon my bosom in lament, and though I try to hold back my tears, they flood my heart. And now, confronted with matters as they are, I wish to let go of the sadness in my heart. Dear soul, please listen to my words, if you can understand them.

Later, Sejong suffered the misfortune of losing his two sons, who also died at a young age. In the 26th year of his reign, the twenty-year old Prince Kwang-pyong suddenly died of abscess. Deeply saddened, the King and Queen went into mourning and fasted for three days. Officials from the Court of Justice and the Secretariat requested that Pae Sang-mun, the Royal Doctor, be put on trial for failing to save the Prince's life. But even amid his sorrow Sejong rejected this proposal from his courtiers, replying, in a manner worthy of a wise king, that since it had been by the hand of fate that his son had died, it could not have been prevented by anyone.

The king's misfortunes mounted further when his seventh son Prince Pyong-won died a month and ten days later. The unexpected deaths of the two princes, within the space of little more than a month, came as a great shock to Sejong. Therefore, two days after the death of Prince Pyong-won, believing that the wrath of Heaven had been provoked by grave miscarriages of justice being carried out in the Provinces, Sejong informed Kim Chong-so of his feelings, together with others, and sent out ordinances to the Governors of the Provinces, sternly reminding them to administer penal laws with justice and fairness. On that day, he also made clear to his courtiers, through Prince Chinyang, that it was his intention to abdicate the throne and hand over the administration of the State to the Crown Prince. His courtiers, moved and alarmed by the King's decision, did their utmost to dissuade him and made clear that they would never accept this command, even if they were to lose their lives. Since his courtiers were adamant, Sejong could do nothing but postpone his abdication.

Spirit of Compassion

Sejong's love for his people was not confined to a particular class. When we consider his warm compassion for the young and old, his concern for the rights of slaves and prisoners, and his policies of welfare and openness to the peoples of other nations, it seems incredible that Sejong inhabited an age in which kings were generally cruel and brutal oppressors of their subjects.

27 November, 12th year

A Royal Ordinance to the Ministry of Justice:

"To be imprisoned and tortured is an ordeal for any man. In the case of children and the elderly, it is pitiful indeed. From this day forward, the detention of those aged below 15 or above 70 is forbidden, unless the charge is one of murder or robbery. Persons below the age of 10 or above the age of 80 shall under no circumstances be detained or beaten, and any verdict passed in their case must be given on basis of many testimonies. Let this Ordinance be known throughout the country, and anyone in breach of it be punished."

24 March, 12th year

A man named Choi Yu-won beat one of his slaves to death. The King ordered the Ministry of Justice to bring him to trial, declaring,

"Even though a man is a slave, he is no less a man, and even if he has sinned, to punish him with death in private and without the sanction of the law is to disregard a master's duty to love and care for his servant. This man's sin should therefore be judged."

19 October, 12th year

The King said to his Secretaries:

"In the past, when a government servant gave birth, she was expected to return to service seven days later. This provision was made out of concern for the fact that harm might come to the baby if she returned leaving the child behind her, and so this period of leave was later increased to a hundred days. However, there have been instances of women whose time was near, and who gave birth before reaching home. I therefore suggest that one month of full leave be granted prior to giving birth. Please amend the relevant laws."

26 April, 16th year
Dispatched to the Ministry of Justice:
"It has been enacted that a female servant, who is due to give birth in a month's time or has given birth within the past hundred days, shall not be required for government service. Since no leave has been granted to the husbands of such women, however, they have not been able to provide assistance to their wives in childbirth, and because of this some women have even lost their lives, which is most pitiful. From this day forward, a husband is not required to return to service for thirty days after his wife has given birth."

28 January, Year 16
Sin Sang, an official from the Ministry of Rites, reported:
"The Alta Tribe of the Jurchens have submitted this message to the Royal Court, 'We understand that you have established a military base in the region of Hwaeryong, and wish to know whether you will allow us to live in peace with you as before, or intend to drive us away.' I believe, Your Highness, that it is their genuine wish to settle with us in peace."
And the king responded:
"If they wish to become part of our nation, we cannot drive them away, and if they wish to leave, there is no need for us to prevent it. Our establishment of a military base will not please them, but it cannot be denied that the rural district of Hwaeryong is our rightful possession. Tongmaeng Kachop Moga [the chief of the Jurchens] once leased the land from us, but

after his tribe was defeated by the rival Oljokhap, the region became desolate and empty, and so now we have been compelled to establish a military camp there to maintain peace. Other Jurchens have settled in Hamgil Province, and if the Alta Tribe wish to come and live in our country, it would be unjust to discriminate against them."

14 May, Year 21

A Royal Message to Kim Chong-so, Commander-in-Chief of the Hamgil Province:

"When the Heavens nourish the earth, they do not distinguish between the great and the small. When a king loves his people, it should be the same."

This message was one of Sejong's injunctions to General Kim, urging him to render aid and support to the nomadic tribes of the North, as though they were the people of his own kingdom.

2 July, 30th year

The King said,

"In the past, I have not been afraid of the heat. As the climate has grown more extreme in recent years, I have begun to soak my hands in water during hot weather. When I do so, the feeling of heat immediately disappears. This has led me to reflect how easy it must be for a man in a prison to be affected by the heat. Some, I believe, even lose their lives because of it, and this is greatly distressing. When there is very hot weather, let us place small jars of water in the cells of the prisons, and replace the water frequently, directing the prisoners to wash their hands so that they are not affected by the heat."

Learning and Diligence

4 August, 5th year

A private order from the King was sent to the Governor of each of the Provinces to send quantities of lacquer tree fruits to Seoul. The oil that is extracted from these fruits burns brightly and without smoke, and could be used for the King's reading at night.

23 December, the 5th year

The King said to a court attendant,

"While I am at the Royal Court, there is never a time when I set my work aside and sit idle."

19 March, 20th year

The King said,

"No classical or historical works have escaped my attention, and although I am now unable to remember with ease due to my age, I do not stop my reading, because as I read, my thoughts are awakened, and many of these thoughts become deeds in my administration of the State. Seen in this light, reading is indeed a source of great benefit."

16 June, 24th year

The King said to several of his Secretaries,

"Ever since I came to the throne, I have thought nothing more worthy of diligent effort than consideration of the affairs of state. Therefore, I have held councils every day to debate and discuss issues of national importance. Through these, I have met with many officials each day, and have given my personal attention to state affairs, dealing with them individually. For this reason, the delivery of sentences has never been delayed, and no important matter has been left unheard."

22 February, 32nd year

The King would rise at dawn every day, and would hear debriefings from his Ministers at daybreak. He would then consider general affairs, and hold council to determine the principles of governance. He would personally interview the governors as they left for their provinces. He participated in *Kyong-yon* in order to reflect upon the Literature of the Sages, and hold discussions about past and present events. Later, he would go to read in the Royal Chamber and would not set down his book until retiring late into the night.

Forgiveness

6th Year, 4 July

The King said,

"Though a crime may justly have incurred the death penalty, if mitigating circumstances can be found, it has always been my way to pardon and forgive it all."

19 April, 7th year,

The King said,

"Appreciation of the good must be long-lasting; hatred for the bad must not."

26 March, 11th year,

The officer Chong Yon said,

"Yesterday, a man leaped out in front of Your Majesty's carriage. According to the laws, he should be executed."

The King replied,

"That is most unjust. If he jumped in full awareness of the law, the rule should be applied as you have said. But to punish an ignorant person who acted out of bewilderment, not knowing his way, is not right.

23, February, the 14th year,

A stray arrow fell into the King's Quarters.

An Sung-son and others said,

"An ordinance forbidding the firing of arrows towards the Palace has been in existence for many years. Although Your Highness is here in person, they have aimed arrows towards the Royal Quarters. This is no minor transgression. Therefore let them stand trial before the court."

The King replied,

"The arrow was fired in competition and it fell here by mistake. Let there be no further investigation of the matter."

25 February, 14th year,

While the King's ostler was on guard in the mountains, a large wild boar, struck with many arrows, managed to break through the fence and charged into the King's Horse, killing it. The officers Choi Yun-dok and Chong Yon declared,

"In their neglect, the palace staffs have allowed the Royal Horse to be killed. We request that Your Majesty permit their offence to be judged."

The King replied,

"It happened quite unexpectedly. How could they have known that a large boar would run into this particular horse? Do not speak of this again."

Frugality

In matters that concerned himself alone, Sejong's conduct was always governed by strict frugality. He would write his commands on paper torn from used government warrants and wore patched and threadbare clothing when not undertaking official business. He also forbade the regional authorities to send local delicacies to him as tribute, concerned that this would be a burden on the people.

7 May, 3rd year

The King had ordered two rooms to be built using discarded timber from the eastern part of the Kyonghoe Hall. The stairways were not be made of stone, the roof was to be covered with straw, and only simple decorations were used, according to the King's request. When the new chambers had been built, he no longer used his old offices, but stayed in these new rooms instead.

11 November, 12th year

Yi Chung-ji of the Ministry of Military Affairs said to the King,

"Your Majesty, the bare appearance of the helmets worn by your carriage escort is unworthy of your dignity. Please grant permission for them to be given lead plating."

To this the King replied,

"Since lead is not a native product of our country, we should not use it for this trivial purpose. Moreover, since the purpose of a soldier's armour is to offer protection, decoration is unnecessary. A light covering of paint and oil will be sufficient.

25 March, 13th year

The King said, "Since I visit the Royal apartments in the Taepyong Quarters only for brief periods of rest, use only rough, unpolished stones when you build the staircase. Save the workman his sweat, and do not burden the people with needless expense."

21 August, 14th year

The courtiers said to the King,

"Your Highness writes Ordinances in a cursive hand on pieces of used warrant paper. While this is economical and concise, it does not appear to us befitting the Royal authority, nor in accordance with the standards of our civilized society. Since Royal Ordinances are usually distributed to every corner of the nation, they should appear in keeping with the authority of the Royal Court, and should be of such cxquisite beauty that the eyes and ears of all are struck with awe, as if the commands came from the heavens themselves. As it is, Your Highness uses only white paper and employs little grandeur in his writing. To the eyes of the ignorant, the Royal Ordinances do not differ greatly from the documents issued by the local authorities, and so fall short of inspiring reverence in the minds of the people."

18 September, 15th year

The King said,

"When I heard that a soldier named Kang In-su was killed while carrying stones for the construction of the new Kangnyong Apartments, I was filled with great remorse. Since coming to the throne of my royal ancestors, I have been able to enjoy the comforts of the Palace, and so ceased to pursue my own wants and fancies. As the Kangnyong chamber was narrow and its roof was leaking, my intention was to make a simple repair, but the work was delayed and is still unfinished. Living in wealth and tranquillity, I should have been grateful and content, and remained in my old house. But in my attempt to have it repaired, a human life has been lost. What use is remorse now? The decision to rebuild the chamber showed my lack of virtue, and now since a person has been killed, my flaws are even clearer than before. I have given a hundred bags of rice to the household of the dead man, but what can be done to help their distress?"

22 January, 19th year

The King said to his secretaries,

"The duty of a king is to love his people. Since the people are now suffering from starvation, it is impossible for me to accept delicacies offered by the provinces. Owing to the bad harvests of last year, the custom of offering delicacies was discontinued in the three southern provinces, and only the Kangwon and Kyonggi provinces continued in their offerings. But now I hear that many are starving to death in Kyonggi, and I am very ashamed. I suggest that we should discontinue the offerings of these two provinces as well."

The secretaries replied,

"Your Majesty, if we put an end to the offerings from these two remaining provinces, we will have no means of providing Your Majesty with meals. If this is Your Highness's wish, we will resort to other means, though we fear that other problems may arise from this. Given, however, that it is your wish, we suggest that we should require offerings to be sent only from the Southern Kyonggi Province, from those districts which have had good harvests."

The King said,

"We cannot discriminate within a single province in this way."

Finally, the King delivered an ordinance,

"With the exception of offerings for the Royal Tomb, all offerings from Kyonggi Province to the Palaces and Government Offices shall be discontinued. Only the ports shall continue as before."

Other Records

The following anecdotes are taken from the writings of many officials and scholars of the Choson period..

A commoner named Cho Won began legal proceedings owing to a dispute over his rice fields. Infuriated by the delays caused by the official responsible for his case, he remarked "The king must be an ignorant man if he has sent such a feckless governor to rule us." The staff of the Court of Justice and officials all pressed for the punishment of Cho Won, but the King ruled against his being put on trial, saying, "Because of the recent flooding and drought, the people have been in great distress. Cho Won's district governor, giving no thought to their sufferings, delayed the final hearing of a lawsuit because he was busy entertaining a personal acquaintance. Cho Won spoke as he did out of resentment at this injustice." And the king refused their request to have him punished. – *Kukjo Pogam* (Precious Mirror of the Government)

The *Sillok* records the same incident:

The Six Ministries and the State Council asserted in the King's presence that Cho Won's case should be tried according to the laws, as a warning to future generations.

The King declared to them,

"On account of the rudeness of his words, you ask for his punishment. This would be appropriate if considered from a purely legal point of view, but I cannot bring myself to punish Cho Won for condemning me. The people have suffered great hardship because of the recent flooding and drought, and yet Cho Won's governor paid no heed to their hardships, but entertained his guest and drank wine, and so delayed the hearing of the dispute over his rice fields. Since Cho Won spoke these words because of this, out of indignation, you should not press for his punishment."

–*Sejong Sillok*, 25 April, 6th year

Yun Hwae and Nam Sumun were among the kingdom's foremost literary scholars, but they loved wine very much and always drank heavily. Sejong, out of admiration and concern for them, ordered them to drink no more than three measures of wine at one sitting. After this, when they were drinking at festive occasions, these men always drank three measures, but used unusually large bowls for each serving. Thus, drinking three bowlfuls, they drank almost twice as much as anyone else. The King, hearing this, smiled and said, "It seems my warning to them has become an encouragement." –*Pirwon Chapgi* (An Author's Trivia' by So Ko-jong)

Choi Chi-un passed the State Examination in the Year of the Fowl (1417) during the reign of King Taejong. He went on to become vice-minister at the Ministry of Personnel, and visited Ming China as an envoy on five occasions. He passed away in the Year of the Ape (1440), at the age of 51. Sejong thought very highly of Choi, and called upon him from time to time to discuss state affairs. Choi would always be consulted whenever an issue of national importance was under consideration. Since by nature he liked to drink, Sejong, out of concern for him, would personally write letters to him to warn him from drinking to excess. One day, Choi fixed these letters to a wall in his house, and repented whenever he saw them, as he left or entered the room. Sometimes, when he came back home very drunk, his wife would make him raise his head and look towards the letters on the wall. Then, even in his drunkenness, he would lower his head on to the desk before him, as if to bow in deep repentance. When sober again, he would say, "I am greatly moved by the King's kindness to me, and always keep in my mind his injunction to guard against excessive drinking. But when I hold a cup of wine in my hand, I immediately forget the warning of the day before and lapse helplessly back into drunkenness." In the end, Choi Chi-wun fell ill because of his drinking, and died shortly after the age of 50. When he was alive, Sejong had commissioned him to write a commentary on *Muwonrok*, a treatise on forensic medicine, and also to provide explanations on various articles of the law. Whenever a difficult case was being tried, Choi's contribution often ensured that a miscarriage of justice was avoided.

–*Somun Soerok* (Collection of Essays and Poems by Cho Sin)

The King was often afflicted by excessive, prolonged periods of thirst. Tae On and others informed him, "According to the Royal Physician, your condition must first be treated with specially prepared food. The flesh of a white rooster, a yellow hen or a lamb are believed to alleviate the feeling of thirst. Therefore, request an official to bring these to Your Majesty every day." Sejong replied, "How can I take away the life of an animal for the sake of my own body? Moreover, lambs are not bred in our country." Tae On and others replied, "There are many lambs raised in the regional government offices. Please agree to our suggestion." But the King would not give permission. *—Yolryosil Kisul* (Collected Works of History by Yi Kung-ik)

The King rarely left the State Chamber, where he reviewed his ideas with the Ministers in order to enable him to govern the country with greater wisdom. Hwang Hui [the Prime Minister] and Ho Cho [the Vice-Prime Minister] were seldom able to remove their official uniform even when they had come out of the Chamber, as they would be summoned there again by the King frequently and at every time of day. *– Chong-am Anthology*

IV. King Sejong's Achievements

1. *Chiphyonjon*, the 'Jade Hall'

Sejong's Devotion to Learning

Since early childhood, Sejong had always loved to read. Once he had read a book, he would read it again a hundred times, and some books, such as *Chwajon* (A biography by Tso Chu-ming) and *Chosa* (Ode of Lamentations by Kulwon), he read over two hundred times until he had learned them by heart. Seeing his son's devotion to reading and study, King Taejong grew anxious for his health and forbade him to read during the night. When his reading continued, Taejong sent an attendant to confiscate and hide all the books in his room. Disheartened, Sejong began to search, and found one book that had escaped the attendant's notice called *Kuso Sugan* (Ou-Su's letters) lying behind a screen. Overcome with joy, he picked it up and proceeded to read it several hundred times. When he learned of this, his father King Taejong said, "Why do you let your body suffer so, as if

The Reading Prince

you were a scholar preparing for the state examination?"

Sejong's desire to learn grew even stronger when he became king and began to attend the *Kyong-yon*, where he learned and discussed Confucian Classics and historical texts with the country's most accomplished scholarly officials. After ascending the throne in July 1418, Sejong began to hold the *Kyong-yon* in October, and attended it as part of his daily routine. After twenty years, Sejong had participated in no fewer than 1,898 of its lectures.

As time passed, however, various problems arose with holding the *Kyong-yon*. The officials in charge of the meeting were still obliged to perform their routine government duties, and as a result often unable to prepare the lectures adequately. Furthermore, the young king's knowledge was already so advanced and his zeal for literature so fervent that the number and depth of the lectures he required were often difficult to provide. A month after the first *Kyong-yon*, for example, Sejong expressed a desire to study *Chachi Tonggam* (A Chronological History of China from BC 403 - AD 959 in 249 volumes). His alarmed courtiers recommended the shorter *Kunsarok* (Confucian philosophy, 4 volumes) on the grounds that *Chachi Tonggam* was too large a work. When Sejong began to read the Brief Study of *Chachi Tonggam* next year, the lack of preparation by his lecturers became even more evident. To solve this problem, Sejong appointed full-time teachers to oversee the *Kyong-yon*, laying the foundations of what eventually grew to become the *Chiphyonjon*, or Jade Hall of Scholars.

The Establishment of *Chiphyonjon*

In response to Sejong's request for the establishment of a royal institute of research, the *Chiphyonjon* or 'Jade Hall' was established within the palace grounds

Scholar's of the Jade Hall

in March, 1420, the second year of his reign.

Ten scholars initially resided there, and later the number grew to twenty. The number increased again to thirty-two when a national project was being undertaken, and returned to twenty after it was completed. As we learn from the *Kukjo Pangmok*, all but one of the scholars who resided at the Jade Hall during the institution's existence had succeeded in the state examination, and just under half were among the top five in their year. They were clearly a very talented group, although very young when they joined the Hall, usually at the age of 23 or 24.

Sejong earnestly supported these scholars in the belief that they were essential to the country's livelihood. As residents of the Hall, they enjoyed many privileges. Sejong ordered the stewards of the Royal Palace to take charge of their meals, providing them on occasions with the kingdom's finest food and drink. The King would often visit the Hall in person to encourage the scholars in their studies. They were also granted exemption from routine administrative duties and the mandatory cycle of offices, as well as special leave for intensive periods of study at home or at Buddhist temples in the mountains.

Once, as the King was taking a quiet walk in the Royal Palace at night, he saw a lamp burning in the Jade Hall, where a scholar named Sin Suk-ju was reading, heedless of sleep. Sejong returned to his room, and ordered one of his servants to observe the scholar's movements. Upon learning from the servant later on that the light had not been put out until dawn, the King went to the Jade Hall and gently placed his *konryongpo* (a regal coat made of silk) over Sin Suk-ju, who was now asleep, and some time after went to bed himself. As soon as the young scholar awoke, he saw the King's coat had been put over his body and had kept him warm all night. Astonished at the King's kindness, he bowed toward the King's chambers with tears in his eyes.

The Purpose of the Jade Hall

Sejong took on many projects in the thirty-two years of his reign, all of which contributed to the welfare of the public, but took many years to complete. The reorganization of the taxation system, for example, took twenty six years and the consolidation of the legislative code seventeen. It was thirty years before the standardization of national ceremonies and the publication of *The History of Koryo* were completed. Even the Korean alphabet took over ten years to bring to its final form. The successful undertaking of so many projects at one time is a remarkable feat, rarely found in the records of history. Sejong was determined to achieve perfection in these projects, and made great use of the intellectual resources available to him at the Jade Hall.

The duties assigned to the scholars ranged widely from purely academic assignments to more active advisory roles in politics. They included the preparation of lectures for the *Kyong-yon*, historical and cultural research, an investigative study of the rituals and institutions of Ancient China, administration of the state examinations, the collection of an extensive library, and the publishing of works of literature deemed important to the state. Of the duties assigned to the Jade Hall scholars, the last was the most demanding. Eighty new books and several hundred pamphlets and reports were published through the *Chiphyonjon* during the reign of King Sejong, covering the subjects of politics, history, literature, linguistics, geography, philosophy, law, music, agriculture, medicine, astronomy, and others. The most noteworthy publications included *Nongsa Chiksol* (A Plain Guide to Farming, 1429), *Taejong Sillok* (The Annals of King Taejong, 1431), *Paldo Chiriji* (The Geographical Descriptions of the Eight Provinces, 1432), *Samgang Haengsildo* (Illustrated Guide to Conduct and the Three Bonds, 1432), *Hyangyak Chipsongbang* (Great Collection of Native Korean Prescriptions, 1433), *Chachi Tonggam Hunie* (Notes on the History of China, 1436), *Hunmin Chongum* (The Proper Sounds to Instruct the People, 1446), *Tongguk Chongum* (Dictionary of Proper Korean Pronunciations, 1447) and *Koryosa* (The History of Koryo, 1450).

The volume and variety of books published through the *Chiphyonjon* demonstrates King Sejong's deep concern with improving the daily life of all his subjects regardless of their class or status through wise government and the study of literature. Though the Jade Hall existed for a relatively short period of thirty six years, it won unparalleled fame for its lasting cultural achievements, which have been an important legacy for the nation of Korea.

2. Development of Legal Institutions

The Purpose of the Laws

Making the laws known to the public

The King said to his ministers, "Even if a man is educated, it is hard for him to appreciate the gravity of an offense until he is sentenced according to the law. How much harder must it be for a less educated man to understand the law and refrain from both major and minor transgressions? Even though it may be impossible for everyone to be acquainted with all the laws, we should at least translate the major articles of law into *Yidu* and display them in public, so that people can avoid falling into criminal ways."

To this, Minister of Justice Ho Jo replied, "I am afraid that this would be a great source of trouble, Your Majesty. Wicked people, if they learn the articles of law, will be afraid of neither light nor heavy crimes, and manipulate the laws to suit their own evil ends."

The King said, "How could it be right to forbid the people to know and understand the laws? To prevent them from knowing a law and to punish them when they break it is itself unjust. My own Royal Ancestors compelled the officials to read out the details of the laws to the people in order that everyone might become familiar with their provisions. Bid the scholars search for such examples in the official records and report them accordingly."

When Ho Jo withdrew, the King said, "According to Ho Jo's way of thinking, if many people become acquainted with the laws, litigation will never cease, and there will be no respect for the officials. But I think it is right to allow the people to know the law, so that they may be careful to avoid violating it."

The King then ordered the Jade Hall scholars to find past examples of the people being made to learn the laws. – *Sejong Sillok*, 7 November, 14th year

Allowing appeals against a judge's decisions

Ho Jo said, "Your Majesty, I fear that by permitting the common people to lodge appeals against a judge's decisions we will impair the distinction between the aristocracy and the lower classes."

The King said, "How could one consider it right to prohibit the weak from voicing their grievances? I understand your objection, but I cannot see that it would be just to do as you say."

When Ho Jo withdrew, the King said to An Sung-son, "Ho Jo is very stubborn."

An said, "Politics is best managed when the people are allowed to reveal their innermost thoughts to those who rule them. As it is written in the *Sogyong* [a Confucian text], 'If the people are unable to live their will and resolve to die instead, the king can attain neither virtue nor happiness, for he will be alone'. What system of government beneath the Heavens can prohibit recompense for grievances and the right of appeal?"

The King smiled and said, "Your words express the thoughts in my heart. From now on, let the officers of law submit to the process of appeal, but enact that Judges may not be punished for their own judgements. This way, we will please both judges and litigants. – *Sejong Sillok*, October,

15th year

These anecdotes illustrate two opposite perspectives on the purpose of law. Ho Jo believed that if the common people became familiar with the law, they would disagree or find faults with decisions given by the judges, and harm would come to the standing and authority of the ruling class. The law was, in his view, no more than a means of controlling the people. For Sejong, it was a means of ensuring that people did not commit wrongful deeds and of preserving the order of society and the happiness of those living within it. For this reason, he sought to increase public awareness of the law and guaranteed his subjects the right to appeal against any unjust decisions. By his final decision to allow appeals to be made while conferring immunity on judges who had allegedly given wrong decisions, Sejong addressed the grievances of the commoners, and at the same time preserved the authority of the officers of law, satisfying both sides.

Revision and Improvement of the Codes

King Taejo, founder of the Choson Dynasty, pronounced on his accession to the throne that a unified code of laws would be established, and the government would be expected to abide by it. Avoiding radical reform, the new regime was to inherit the laws of the former Koryo dynasty. So it was that the Six Codes of Governance were established under Taejo, and the Supplemental Six Codes were added during the reign of Taejong and Sejong. Subsequently, the National Code, initiated by Sejo and completed under Songjong, became the foundation of Choson Dynasty now governed by the rule of law.

Sejong believed in the beneficent nature of the law as a means of protecting people, and attempted in every way possible to ensure that its provisions were appropriate and effective. Whenever a new law was enacted, he would examine precedents in the ancient legal codes to be certain that it did not contradict them. At the same time, he would consider the reaction of the people to the new law, and how likely they were to accept it as reasonable. Once a new law was established, it could not be easily modified or revoked unless certain conditions were met.

Whilst he considered that the law should be essentially stable and unchanging, Sejong always kept foremost in his mind the comfort and well-being of the people. The following quotations, taken from the *Sejong Sillok*, illustrate this.

"The best law is an ancient law. But even if a law is very old, if the people dislike it, it should be removed."

"When enacting a law, one should not think of oneself, but of the public good first. If each man enacts laws for his own benefit, the corruption will spread to the people."

And above all,

"Laws should be founded on compassion and morality."

Reform of the Criminal Justice System

The criminal justice system become steadily more chaotic since the end of the Koryo period, and when Sejong came to the throne, it was plagued by officials who meted out cruel punishments and illegal tortures with little regard for human life. Sejong was deeply concerned that the majority of judicial officers were giving judgment on a subjective basis, rather than on grounds of evidence obtained through proper investigation, and that many mistakes and failures were taking place within the justice system. Thus, in the thirteenth year of his reign, he composed and dispatched a letter of almost four thousand words, urging officers throughout the country to give fair and carefully measured verdicts.

Though he was eager that trials should be carried out fairly, Sejong's ultimate aspiration was a country which could exist without a penal system, and a harmonious society whose prisons were all empty. Faced in reality with circumstances that required penal laws, Sejong often agonized greatly over verdicts he was called to deliver, and would often lighten punishments as far as possible whenever he could. To reinforce the moral fabric of society, he improved the procedure for appeal and regulated the punishment system. The most important items of his reforms were as follows:

1. In the case of offenses for which a specific legal provision is not available, the judge was to apply analogous laws with caution. When passing sentence, the death penalty was to be avoided if at all possible, and lighter punishments applied with less severity.

2. The rod used for official beatings was made according to standardized measurements, and the striking of certain important parts of the body, such as the backbone, was forbidden.

3. In the case of crimes for which a fine could be paid in place of a punishment, the fines were reduced, and the lower classes were allowed to pay lesser fines.

4. The Law of Three Appeals: those accused of capital crimes were to be granted three opportunities for appeal to the king, so that none would die with an unheard grievance.

5. Convicted women who were pregnant would begin to serve their sentence only 100 days after giving birth.

6. Except in cases of murder or robbery, those below the age of 15 or above the age of 70 were not to be imprisoned. Those below the age of 10 or above the age of 80 were not to be imprisoned under any circumstances.

7. Those sentenced to penal servitude whose parents were above the age of 70 served their sentence in the region where their parents were living.

8. Officials guilty of accepting bribes of any kind were no longer to be pardoned.

9. When a slave-owner beat or killed his slave in private, he was to be punished according to the law.

10. Constant efforts were made to ensure that none were placed in custody for an unduly long period of time because of delays in the legal process.

11. Designs for new prisons were drawn up under the King's supervision, and construction of them begun across the country. Separate prisons were built for women and men, cooler prisons for spring and summer, and warm prisons for the fall and winter period. Prisoners were also allowed to bathe once a week.

3. Reform of the Land Tax

The land tax was the largest source of revenue to the national treasury during the Choson dynasty. During King Sejong's reign, this land tax system underwent several major reforms, and it was over seventeen years before it was completed and fully amended.

When Sejong came to the throne, farmers were obliged to give a tenth of their yearly harvest to the government. The tax inspectors were expected to take into account the quality of the year's harvest and adjust the percentage to be paid accordingly. However, corrupt inspectors would often take advantage of the system to enrich themselves at the expense of the taxpayers. As a result, the farmers were often forced to pay too much tax, while revenues to the national treasury declined. To address this problem, Sejong proposed a new system, under which an average would be taken of the harvests of recent years, and the tax calculated on this basis – a flat-sum system of taxation, in other words. Even though he could have forced the law through immediately, Sejong spent the entire first half of his reign considering the wisdom of his new proposal, since he wanted the system of taxation to be realistic and fair to both the state and the people.

The new system was implemented after the public had been consulted and lengthy discussions had taken place within the government, and the legislation tested for oversights and other problems. The reforms were innovative and revolutionary both in their preparation and execution. The following is a brief summary of the review process to which the reforms were subjected before their implementation.

1. In 1430, a nationwide survey was conducted to gauge public opinion regarding the introduction of flat-sum taxation. A total of 170,000 people, including farmers and court officials, participated in the survey.

2. Officials and scholars reported the reasons which had been put forward in favor of the form and against it, as gathered in the survey. The King took part in lively debates with past and present high-ranking officials concerning these findings.

3. A Land Tax Reform Committee was established to refine the new scheme and take measures to avoid potential difficulties.

4. A trial of the new system began in the Cholla province, and from there the new system gradually spread to the rest of the country.

The main argument against flat-sum taxation was that it was contrary to the interests of the poor, who were more likely to own less fertile land. Those backing the reform, however, argued that the existing structure was too readily exploited by the corrupt officials, whose policy of awarding large rebates in return for bribes was threatening to bankrupt the public treasury. To combat such problems, they contended, a flat system of taxation, which levied revenues on an objective basis, was needed.

Even though the surveys, official reports, and court discussions had revealed substantial support for the reform, King Sejong continued to deliberate on the matter. For it weighed on his mind that much of the support for the reform had come from the harvest-rich South. Sejong therefore deferred its implementation for six years, during which time he sought to address the problem that less fertile land might be subject to relatively heavy taxes, as well as other difficulties that might arise during times of bad harvest. It was only when the system received unanimous approval at court, even from Hwang Hui and Maeng Sa-song, who had originally opposed the reform, that the new system was brought into effect in the year 1444.

This final system divided the land into six categories, according to its fertility, and the quality of the harvest into nine grades. It was now possible to take into account the differences in productivity between each of the regions, as well as changes in climate. The new scheme was incorporated into the National Codes, and served as a basis for the taxation system in the remaining years of the Choson dynasty.

4. Music: A Joy to Share with the People

King Sejong was a great lover of music, and from his relationship with Pak Yon, the most talented musician of the Choson Dynasty, came many of the great advances in the music of 15th century Korea. It was a relationship that went beyond that of monarch and courtier. As far as music was concerned, they were friends, and from their debates and discussions, were able to learn much from one another and gain much inspiration.

Sejong instructed Pak to find a method for the tuning of all musical instruments. If this were found, existing instruments could be improved, new ones could be invented, and a complete Korean orchestra could be assembled. Just as in Western classical music, instruments are only able to play together when they have been harmonized to a certain level of tuning. An accurate standard of tuning is therefore very important for the music of any nation or culture. After many failures, Pak Yon finally succeeded in establishing the twelve standard notes by creating a pitch-pipe called the *Hwangjongwan*. He went on to develop and improve fifty six musical instruments and make nine new ones.

Among the instruments used in the Royal Court of Choson Korea was a set of sixteen stone chimes called the *Pyon-gyong*. Since it was made of stone, its tuning or 'tone-color' would not change easily, even in times of high humidity or sudden variances in temperature. The *Pyon-gyong* was therefore always used as the standard of tuning for any musical piece in which it featured. It was, however, made of jade stone, which was not native to Korea. Consequently, the stone often had to be imported from China, or a clay version of the instrument was built and used as a substitute. In either case, the instrument was not generally very well tuned.

In the autumn of 1426, the seventh year of Sejong's reign, a quantity of jade stone was discovered at Namyang, Kyonggi Province. It was beautiful and gave out a pure, clear sound when struck. Over the next three years, it was possible to make a further 528 of the component chimes needed to build the *Pyon-gyong*. The official records attribute the discovery of the stone to the grace of the Heavens, moved to aid a noble king who harbored a genuine desire to help the music of his country develop and improve.

One day Pak Yon gave a performance with a *Pyon-gyong* he had built using the recently discovered jade. After listening to the demonstration, King Sejong said, "The tuning of the Chinese *Pyon-gyong* was imprecise, but your tuning has been done very well. The new jade is indeed a fortunate discovery. The sound that comes from this stone is clear and beautiful, and the tuning is almost perfect. However, the *ichik* is a little too high." The *ichik*, or *G#* in Western musical terms,

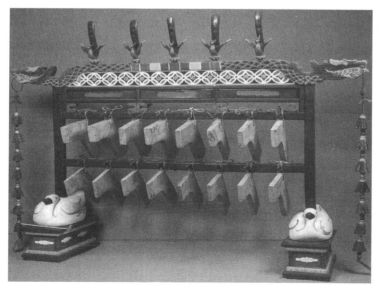

Pyon-gyong

was the 9th note of the scale, and King Sejong was pointing out a slight deviation in its tuning. Surprised, Pak Yon retired from the King's presence and examined each stone in detail. Just as the King had observed, the *ichik* was incorrectly tuned.

When the *Pyon-gyong* was being made, a "ㄱ" shape was drawn on the stone using ink, and the mason was expected to cut along the marked line. Some of the ink marking Pak had originally made on the stone was still visible, and had as a result produced a higher pitch than intended. Having ground away the layer of stone still marked by the ink, he was able to tune it to the correct level. As a result of this incident, Pak Yon came to revere and esteem Sejong even more greatly.

Sejong was also a composer of music. The *Sejong Sillok* gives us a picture of the King at work: "Being familiar with tuning, all the new music has been of the King's making. Tapping the ground with a stick, he would compose a piece in a single day." (11 December, 31st year)

Sejong and Pak Yon between them composed a total of two hundred new musical pieces. Among these, Sejong's personal compositions included the *Chongdaeop* (Great Achievements), *Potaepyong* (Preservation of Peace) and *Pongraeui* (Phoenix). These were pieces written for large-scale performances combining instrumental music with singing and dance. *Chongdaeop* and *Potaepyong* consisted of eleven movements, the smaller *Pongraeui* of seven. The *Yominrak* (A Joy to Share with the People) movement from the *Pongraeui* remains a standard item in the repertoire of traditional Korean orchestras today. *Chongdaeop* and *Potaepyong* are played at memorial ceremonies for the Kings of the Choson Dynasty.

Since a means of writing down the new music was lacking, Sejong created a new form of musical notation known as *Chongganbo*. It consisted of blocks of cells in the shape of a well, resembling the Chinese character 井, and in the cells the names of the notes were written. Since no other system of mensural notation[2] capable of recording both the pitch and length of a note existed at this time even in China, its introduction by King Sejong marked the beginning of a new era in the history of Asian music.

Towards the end of the 9th century, musical notation in Europe was expressed by the neume system[3]. By the closing years of the 12th century, the newly-invented

Chongganbo

---

2 A system which gave notes fixed rhythmic values, making it possible for complex rhythms to be expressed with greater exactness and flexibility.

3 Neumes were the basic elements of Western systems of musical notation prior to the invention of staff notation. They were typically inflective marks, indicating the general shape of a line of music, but not necessarily conveying the exact notes or rhythms to be sung.

'square notation' made it possible to express the length of a note more clearly. Passing through the hands of countless musicians, it evolved into the five-line staff notation we use today. It is surprising that a method of notation capable of recording both pitch and length was established in Korea in so comparatively short a period of time. Thanks to the system of *Chongganbo*, many musical pieces of the early Choson period have survived to be enjoyed by Koreans for many centuries. The *Chongganbo*, as it was originally set out by King Sejong, has been passed down to us in the *Sejong Sillok*, and, alongside the modern five-line notation, is still widely used in Korean music today.

5. Sejong's Contribution to Medical Science

The limited material that survives from the Koryo and early Choson periods indicates that the population grew at an annual rate of 0.1% before the 13th century, but that it had gradually increased to more than 0.4% by the time of the 15th century. It is likely that one of the reasons for this fourfold increase was the significant progress made in Korean medicine during this period. Until the 12th century, Korea was far behind China in its medical knowledge and expertise. Later, however, as Korean scientists began to carry their medical research further, with a strong emphasis on drugs derived from indigenous sources, Korea was soon able to rival China with its discoveries and advances.

Since the beginning of the 15th century, the study of medicinal herbs had been a separate branch of academic study, and King Sejong's active support contributed to the success in many research projects carried out in this field. In order to lay foundations for the systematic development of medical science, Sejong planned the publication of exhaustive work on Korean medicine. In preparation for it, he sent medical researchers abroad to study the most-celebrated foreign treatises written on the subject of medicinal plants, so that they could begin their own studies equipped with all the knowledge currently available. Meanwhile, the details of local drugs prepared and used throughout the country were collected and subjected to refinement. The year 1433, the 15th of Sejong's reign, finally saw the publication of *Great Collection of Native Korean Prescriptions*. A total of 703 medicinal ingredients were covered in this book, including 374 herbs, 109 minerals, and 220 animal products – at a time when only herbs were being used as medicine in Europe. It is also noteworthy that this book, which included treatments for 959 types of illness, not only cites Korean medical works, but also material taken from over 160 medical documents from the Han, Tang, Sung, and Yuan dynasties of China. Each entry specifies the symptoms and the cure for a specific disease, and features with it the original text from which the information was taken, and the regions and seasons in which the medication could be obtained.

In 1445, a joint effort by the Jade Hall scholars and medical experts culminated in the publication of a medical encyclopedia of 365 volumes, entitled *Uibang Yuchwi* (A Classified Collection of Medical Prescriptions). Its opening pages include a preface, explanatory notes, bibliography, table of contents, and an index of the prescribed treatments dealt with in the work. The introduction explains the method of diagnosis and prescription, the principles of healing and cure, directions for the taking of medicine, the desirable qualities of a doctor, and the properties of individual drugs, together with their methods of preparation. The main body of the text comprises 90 chapters, which deal separately with internal disorders, surgery, ophthalmology, otorhinolaryngology (the study of ear, nose and throat diseases), oralogy, dermatology, gynecology, pediatric diseases and acute infectious diseases. The work also contains 153 medical treatises, including 40 Chinese texts which would otherwise have been lost, making the work an important historical source for the study of oriental medicine. It is likely to have been due to the knowledge provided by the manuals in this encyclopedia that there was a noticeable decline in the infant mortality rate and overall rise in population growth at this time.

Another contribution made by King Sejong to the development of medical science in Korea was in the field of forensic medicine, which seeks to ascertain the causes and the means whereby an injury or death has occurred. If general medicine is practiced for the sake of extending human life and preserving health, forensic medicine is studied out of respect for human rights, to ensure that they are not violated.

According to documentary evidence, post-mortem examinations first began in Korea during Sejong's reign. Particularly in cases of homicide, Sejong emphasized the importance of thorough investigation and informed judgment, so that the victim did not suffer injustice. The governor in whose district the crime had occurred would be first to inspect the corpse. Regardless of his findings, the governors of neighbouring districts would then hold independent inquests, up to the number of six, at the place where the dead body had been found. It was also permissible for particularly complex cases to be brought to the Royal court for the sake of appeal.

Autopsy guidelines were printed in *Sinju Muwonrok* (Newly Annotated Coroner's Manual) and distributed to all the judicial authorities. Based on the world's first forensic medical text *Sewonrok* (published in China in 1247) and its revised version *Muwonrok* (1303), *Sinju Muwonrok* was Choson Korea's first manual of forensic medicine, made possible for use in Korea by the addition of detailed notes. The work consisted of two volumes, the first dealing with the laws and regulations concerning autopsies, including sample cases, and the second explaining the methods for ascertaining the cause of death by the signs of injury. Strange as it may seem, the detailed and scientific *Sinju Muwonrok*, although written in the 15th century, is still considered sophisticated by the standards of modern forensic science as practiced today.

6. Innovations in Printing

Printing has a long history in Korea. The method of printing using wooden blocks (xylography) began in the 8th century, and movable metal type (typography) was used for the first time in 1234, some two hundred years before Gutenberg developed his famous printing press in Germany. The first book in the world to be printed using metal type was *Sangjong Kogum Yemun*, published in Korea in 1234. The oldest remaining example of a volume published using movable metal print is *Jikji Simgyong*, published by the Hungdok Temple in 1377. In recognition, UNESCO has established the 'Jikji Memory of the World Prize', which is awarded to individuals and institutions that have made significant contributions to the preservation and accessibility of historical documentation. Korea's metal type technology spread into China, and in 1313 the Mongolian Yuan dynasty began to produce type using tin. Later, this technology would spread further into Arabia and Europe, and so prepare the way for the modern printing press.

The technique of wooden block printing had been subject to constant refinement since the Koryo Dynasty (AD 918-1392) and reached its highest stage of development in Sejong's reign. However, movable type printing, which was more economical in labour, cost, and space, was still in its early stages and operating at a relatively low level of efficiency. The *Kyemi* font (1403), for example, invented under King Taejong, was designed in a wedge shape, and was used to embed the type-letters in a wax tablet. The wax was supposed to hold the type in place as the sheets were pressed on to it, but they generally became loosened in the process, and the printer often had to stop to reset the type. Such interruptions restricted the frequency with which copies could be made with this method.

Sejong felt it was necessary to improve typography in order to meet the demand for a great number and variety of printed texts. He directed his technicians to look into new ways of keeping the type in place during the printing process. After a long period of research and many failed experiments, they succeeded in creating a new font called *Kyongja*, made possible by an idea which had suddenly occurred to the King during the testing process. "Instead of using a soft material such as wax," he suggested, "Why do we not set the type on top of copper plates, fixed to one another?" The new font created in this way had a flat heel instead of a pointed one, and the cuboid type was held in place by lengths of bamboo and secured with recycled paper. The result was a printing process that was not only more economical, but faster, with a printing run of up to 100 copies per day, a five-fold improvement in efficiency on the former models.

Sejong encouraged his technicians to improve type-face design as well. The new *Kyongja* font had greatly improved the speed of printing, but the type it used was very small and dense (10×11mm), and the letters gave a sharp, rigid impression on the page. Sejong directed his technicians to redesign the type, and a new font, covering two hundred thousand characters, was created by Yi Chon, Chong Cho, Kim Ton, Kim Pin, Chang Yong-sil and others. Before the invention of Hangul by Sejong, Koreans wrote using Chinese characters. Since Chinese is an ideographic language, the number of characters is very large indeed. The newly-designed *Kabin* font (14×15mm) was by far the most popular type-face of the Choson Period, and was recast seven times before the 19th century.

The King was also responsible for the invention of a variety of lead-based metal type. He wanted to produce large-type publications for the elderly, whose failing eyesight made it difficult for them to read characters of standard size. He and his technicians were aware that lead had a low melting point and cooled quickly, and was consequently well suited to be used for casting type. The *Pyongjin* font (22×30mm) was created in 1436 and used to print, amongst other volumes, the *Chachi Tonggam Kangmok* (A Brief Study of History of China).

Even after Sejong had raised the standard of metal type to a much higher level, the wood-block technology was still used. This was due to the differing needs of the academics and the people. Metal type printing was reserved for texts of specialist interest and new literature on emerging fields of academia required by scholars, as well as for elaborate and luxurious books, since these tended to be in less demand. Wood-block printing, on the other hand, was used for books aimed at mass circulation, on ethics, the teachings of the sages, the calendars, and essential manuals for farmers. In other words, metal type was the natural choice for printing many different kinds of books in smaller quantities, while the wooden press was more suited to large-scale printing. Wood-blocks, once carved, could continue to be used to reproduce a certain text for as long as they were properly preserved.

Ensuring a source of good quality paper was a key element in the King's drive to improve printing technology. Sejong encouraged the cultivation of *takji* (paper mulberry), which had existed in Korea since the period of the Three Kingdoms (BC 57 (?)-AD 676). It had been considered valuable by Chinese scholars since the time of the Sung dynasty (AD 960-1279) for its fine quality. But as the demand for *takji* paper was beginning to exceed supply, Sejong decided to develop alternative varieties of paper, experimenting with materials such as rice straw, cotton, bamboo, and hemp.

Sejong also ensured that the actual process of publishing was improved and maintained at a high level. To enhance the appearance of the ink on the paper, he decreed punishments for careless workers who were found responsible for lapses in its quality. Strict measures were also taken to eliminate typesetting errors. Both the

Publications during Sejong's reign

Subject	Metal Type	Wooden Print	Unpublished
Pronunciation of Chinese Characters	3	3	1
Music	2	1	6
Ritual	1	2	5
Literature	6	7	3
Foreign Languages	5	0	0
Chinese Literature	27	10	0
Agriculture	2	5	0
Medicine	7	14	1
Korean History	7	0	8
Chinese History	21	4	0
Chinese Classics	15	27	0
Buddhism	2	19	0
Education	4	17	0
Laws	10	6	1
Arts of War	2	6	0
Chinese Laws	4	6	1
Astronomy	1	16	4
Calendars	0	32	0
Mathematics	1	3	1
Geography and Maps	1	3	7
Dictionary	0	3	0
Calligraphy	0	5	0
Total	114	194	40

proof-reader and the 'topper' or technician responsible for ensuring that each folio page was produced on a level printing surface, were required to inspect and sign the proof sheets, and to check also for illegible characters. If they overlooked any errors, they could be punished. Such care meant that the books published during King Sejong's reign among the best-produced in all antiquity.

Whenever a book was published, Sejong would hold a great feast in his delight. Through his earnest desire to share the blessings of culture and literature with many, the art of printing in 15th century Korea took many great steps forward.

7. Developments in Agriculture

Publication of *A Plain Guide to Farming*

The economy of Choson Korea was heavily dependent on farming. The end of the Koryo dynasty saw the beginning of a period of strong growth in the Korean population. For this reason, Sejong sought to increase agricultural productivity by raising the standard of the methods commonly used to cultivate the land. He was particularly concerned about the crude and unsophisticated techniques employed in the northernmost provinces of Pyongan and Hamgil, and commissioned a group of officials to report on the methods of more advanced provinces who enjoyed greater productivity (*Sejong Sillok*, 13 July, 10th year).

> Though the land is fertile in both the provinces of Hamgil and Pyongan, since the people who live there are barely acquainted with the newer methods of farming, they continue as they have always done, and do not produce as much as they are able to. It is my hope to gather knowledge of many effective farming techniques and make them known to the farmers of Hamgil and Pyongan. Therefore, inquire among the experienced farmers in Kyongsang Province about their methods of tilling, sowing, weeding, harvesting, and crop rotation, and discover also the nature of soil appropriate for the five main varieties of crop. Bring together their knowledge and experience, and then publish your findings.

Obeying his command, the local governors of the southernmost provinces of Chungchong, Kyongsang and Cholla all conducted interviews with experienced elderly farmers in their separate regions. The greater part of their findings were then sent to the Jade Hall, where scholars such as Chong Cho and Pyon Hyomun distilled key particulars of the agricultural techniques then practiced in the most developed parts of the nation. They published the final version in May, 1429, calling the work *A Plain Guide to Farming*.

> The practice of farming is of fundamental importance to all who live beneath the Heavens, and from times of old, no wise king has allowed it to escape his attention. Since the weather is different in all of the five zones [East, West, North, South, Center], there is an appropriate way to plant and cultivate in each region. Therefore, since the farming manuals of the past cannot be used unquestioningly, inspectors have been sent to visit old farmers and learn from them methods that have been proven successful through long use and practice. After that, editors removed from the findings all unnecessary repetitions, and so extracted the essential points of instruction, gathering all the knowledge in a single volume entitled *A Plain Guide to Farming*. A work concerned entirely with agricultural technique, it is intended to be concise and accurate so that even remote peoples who live in mountain dwellings may easily understand it.
>
> - The Preface, *A Plain Guide to Farming*

Chong Cho, the chief editor of the work and the author of this preface, believed that farming methods should correspond to the natural features of the region in which they were used, and should also be practical enough for even the least educated of people to put to use easily.

A Plain Guide to Farming set out the basics of farming practices, including guidelines for preparing seeds to be sown the following year and for breaking up the soil before sowing them. It also explained methods for cultivating and harvesting the major crops, such as hemp, rice, millet, soy bean, red bean, green gram, barley, wheat, sesame, and buckwheat. The methods for using different fertilizers, such as human manure, ashes, cattle dung, and stable refuse, are also dealt with. Lastly, it introduced the reader to the various tools of farming, such as the plough, rake, harrow, *bunji* (a board with a string handle, used for levelling the soil), mallet (for breaking up earth or covering seeds), trowel, and hoe.

The entries which explain the practice of tilling the land before sowing and the importance of using sufficient fertilizer are particularly interesting, since they enabled farmers to cultivate the same field continuously from year to year. From today's perspective, it may seem strange that this was not generally the case, but in ancient and medieval times when chemical-based fertilizers did not exist, farmers had little choice but to wait for one or two years until the soil had returned to a reasonable level of productivity. This was also the case in Western Europe, where farmers generally employed a three-year rotation technique, allowing the soil to lie fallow for a further year in order to replenish it.

In the early days of the Choson dynasty, Korean farmers adopted a more intensive approach to cultivation, as this was the only way to support the rapidly increasing population. A considerable amount of fertilizer was required for the land to retain its capacity to grow more crops, and the editors of *A Plain Guide to Farming* devoted a great portion of the work to the preparation and correct use of various fertilizers.

For farmers unable to obtain enough fertilizer, an alternative was to plant different kinds of crop in successive years. Crops such as wheat and barley, for example, require large amounts of nitrogen and phosphoric acid. If they are planted in late autumn or early spring, and their roots are pulled up after the harvest to be used as fertilizer, crops such as soy or red bean, which absorb nitrogen from the atmosphere by means of the bacteria in their roots, can be planted in their place. In this way the soil is replenished and the land can be used continuously.

Another resourceful farming technique is found in the discussion of tilling. According to the *Guide*, the speed with which soil nutrients were restored is largely dependent on the method of ploughing used. *A Plain Guide* explains the various techniques of ploughing in great detail, as well as the correct times to use them. In spring and summer, for example, it states that one should not plough too deeply, whereas in autumn the furrow should be as deep as possible.

The Invention of the Rain Gauge

As the trend towards continuous farming grew, Sejong was keen to determine the levels of rain which were falling in the various parts of his kingdom. Knowing these levels would make it possible to estimate how much water would be available in the streams and reservoirs in each district for farmers, and the effect this would have on the crop yields in those areas.

Though it is uncertain when it became a standard procedure, the technique of measuring rainfall remained almost unchanged from the days of the Koryo dynasty into the Choson period. The depth to which rainwater seeped into the ground was measured using this method, and then reported to the Ministry of Finance, where regular records were kept. The record was valuable as it was based on observable data, but it was far from accurate in terms of scientific measurement, since the depth to which rainwater penetrates is dependent on many other potentially distorting factors.

In the year 1441, a more precise method for measuring precipitation appeared with the invention of the rain gauge, a milestone in the history of meteorology. The new metallic, circular gauge was an invention of the Crown Prince, and developed in collaboration with other scientists. Measuring 42.5cm in height and 17cm in diameter, it was the first device in the world capable of measuring levels of rainfall accurately, preceding Benedetto Castelli's pluviometer by almost 200 years.

The original model of the rain gauge was made in the autumn of 1441, but after a number of defects were discovered during testing, further modifications had to be made. The smaller second model, measuring 31.9cm in height and 14.9cm in diameter, made it possible to perform measurements using smaller amounts of rain, and was officially presented on May 8th of the following year, under the name of *Chugugi*. Replicas of the model were distributed to all local authorities, together with detailed instructions on how to make and use the device. The regulations concerning the rain gauge, as enacted in 1442, were as follows:

1. The rain gauge *Chugugi* is a device of iron composition.
2. Its height is 1 *cha* 5 *chi* [31.9cm.], and its diameter 7 *chi* [14.9cm].
3. Measurements should be taken after the rain has stopped falling.
4. The water level is measured by means of the *chuchok* [a ruler].
5. The date of the rainfall and the time at which it begins and ends should be recorded.
6. The level of rainwater should be measured accurately, to the smallest units of *cha*, *chi* and *pun*.
7. The Hall of Heavenly Records must report the measurements immediately.

The measurements were reported as follows: "In the month of [ ], at the [ ] hour, in the [ ] part the day, there was light rainfall. The level of water taken by the *Chugugi* was [ ] *cha*, [ ] *chi*, [ ] *pun*". In this way, the scientists of 15th century Korea were able to adopt a more scientific approach to meteorology by taking quantitative measurements of natural phenomena, recording them systematically, and analyzing them statistically.

8. Astronomy and Inventions

The studies in astronomy undertaken during the reign of Sejong were originally initiated by the King in order to determine the latitude of the nation's capital, Seoul. In July 1432, when discussing the theory of the calendar with his scholar officials in a meeting of the *Kyong-yon*, Sejong realized that it would be necessary to develop astronomical instruments in order to verify the exact position of Seoul's northern extremity. *Ta-tungryok*, the Chinese almanac then commonly in use, had naturally been calculated from the perspective of Beijing, and this led to errors when used in Korea, because of time differences. There was therefore a need for a new almanac, with Seoul as its primary point of reference. Sejong commissioned two scholars, Chong Cho and Chong In-ji to investigate the theory and workings of *Kanui* devices by consulting the existing literature on the subject. *Kanui*, for which the closest English equivalent is the word 'Torquetum', was a device which enabled measurements to be made in three sets of co-ordinates, horizontal, equatorial and ecliptic, and could thus be used to determine the latitude of Seoul. Sejong ordered Yi Chon and Chang Yong-sil to take charge of the construction of these astronomical instruments. Their first attempt was a wooden prototype, built as part of a pilot project, which determined the northern extremity of Seoul to be 38°N, corresponding with the figure reported by the *Ta-tungryok*. Having gained confidence, Sejong and his scientists began to design and construct a more refined version of the instrument using copper.

As the production of the second *Kanui* neared completion, Sejong ordered Minister An Sun to build an observatory to the north of the Kyonghi Hall to house the new device. So it was that in 1434, the largest observatory in Asia since the Kwansong Observatory of Yuan China was built in the grounds of Royal Palace. It was 6.5m high (21.33 ft), 9.9m long (32.48 ft), and 6.7m wide (21.98 ft). To the west of the Kanui Observatory stood the *Kyupyo*, which were stone pillars overlaid with copper. Marks for the unit measurements *chang, chok, chon, pun* were inscribed on a slab of azure stone which lay on the ground, and measured the length of the shadow cast by the pillars. By taking the length and position of the shadow, the time and even the 24 solar-terms could be calculated with accuracy. Two smaller, portable versions of the *Kanui* were also built, one of them kept at Chonchu Hall and the other at Soungwan (Hall of Heavenly Records).

Under Sejong's direction, four different types of sundial were made, of varying shapes and functions. Amongst these, the most famous was the *Angbu Ilgu* or cauldron-sundial. The *Angbu Ilgu*, an astronomical device unique to Korea was built in a concave hemisphere like a cauldron, with lines drawn inside to measure the time of day and the 24 solar-terms. The gnomon, a raised arm fixed to one side

of the concave surface, indicated the time by its shadow. Since the height of the sun changed throughout the year, being higher in summer and lower in winter, the changes in the seasons could be discerned from the location of the shadow along the solar-term lines. In order to make the sundial accessible to those who were illiterate, Sejong had the animal symbols for each hour drawn on to the dial's surface.[4] He then had it installed

Sundial *Angbu Ilgu*

---

[4] At that time in Asia, each day was divided into twelve hours, and the twelve hours were represented by twelve animals: rat, ox, tiger, rabbit, dragon, snake, horse, goat, monkey, chicken, dog, and pig.

on the street to the south of the Royal Ancestral Shrine, for use as a public clock.

But since the sundial could not be used during the night, Sejong ordered his technicians to make the *Ilsong Chongsiui* (literally: 'Fixed time piece of sun and star'), which was able to keep time during the night as well. Four such clocks were made, one of which was installed in the Hall of Heavenly Records, another in the east of Manchun Hall, and the other two in border regions. Additionally, Sejong gave a special order for a portable sundial to be made for use by the frontier garrisons.

The most well-known water clock in Korean history is the *Chagyongnu*, invented by Chang Yong-sil in 1434. Along with its inventor, the water clock is so well celebrated in Korea that it is known even to little children, and its picture appears on the 10,000 won bill. Unlike other water clocks, it had the capacity both to display and announce the time to those nearby. Bells, cymbals and drums would sound according to the passing of *si*, *kyong* and *chom* (the traditional Asian time units), and a mechanical doll would also emerge to tell the time.

Water Clock *Chagyongnu*

The *Sejong Sillok* (1 June, 16th year) records in detail the structure and mechanics of the *Chagyongnu*: "It contained four water containers of varying sizes filled with water and two containers into which the water flowed. As the water levels rose in the latter containers, a spring device was triggered, causing an iron ball to be released, which would in turn activate the sound mechanism. A bell would ring to represent the passing of *si* [a unit of time equal to 1/12th of a day], a drum would sound for *kyong* [a unit equal to 1/5th of period between 7pm and 5am] and a cymbal for the *chom* [equivalent to one hour]."

Sejong installed the water clock in the Poru Tower, which had been built to the south of the Kyonghi Pavilion for this special purpose. Chang Yong-sil, who received much praise from King Sejong for this invention, went on to build another water clock called *Okru*, which had greater precision than former models. The *Okru* was housed in Humgyong Tower, next to the King's chambers, in order to enable the King to visit it frequently. While the *Chagyongnu* and the *Ongnu* water clocks were both automatic devices, the *Ongnu* was more sophisticated, as it also displayed the positions and movements of the stars and the planets.

As well as overseeing the design of many new observational instruments, King Sejong was also concerned with the actual observation of the sky. He despatched scholars to various mountains in the peninsula in order to observe solar eclipses, a remarkable and almost unknown command for a monarch of the Choson dynasty to issue. In March 1428, Sejong ordered So Wun-jong, Pak Yom and others to climb the Samgak mountain in Seoul, as the eclipse which had been predicted to occur at the dawn of the following day could not be seen from a low altitude. Four years later, in December 1432, Sejong ordered a three-story observatory to be built on the Samgak Mountain, so that researchers at the Hall of Heavenly Records would be able to observe the rising and setting of the sun there.

Other records show that staff from the Hall of Heavenly Records were despatched to Mt. Mani, Mt. Paekdu, and Mt. Halla in order to calculate the latitude of the North Star. Researchers were also sent to the observatory at Kumgang Mountain, showing that astronomical observations were carried out in the very farthest reaches of the peninsula. According to the *Sillok*, nineteen solar eclipses were observed and recorded during Sejong's reign alone. Many other records of astronomical observations have survived, including records of the eclipse of planets by the moon (12), the eclipse of fixed stars by planets (13), the approach and overlap of planets (2), the appearance of novas and comets (14), sun's corona and white rainbows (359), shooting stars (30), and stars seen during the day (66).

When a celestial irregularity such as a solar or lunar eclipse occurred in Choson Korea, the King held a ceremony called the *Kusikrae*, which signified his obedience to Heaven's will and a pledge to rule with caution and wisdom. Confucian thought, which exerted considerable influence on Korean society, put emphasis on the importance of harmony between man and nature, and the *Kusikrae* was therefore a very important ceremony. Astronomical staff carefully observed heavenly phenomena and changes in the behaviour of stars and planets, so that the King could be warned of an eclipse at least three months in advance in order to prepare for the ceremony. The hour in which the eclipse would occur was the most vital piece of information, but the forecast was also required to be correct to the minute and even the second. If not, the officials of Hall of Heavenly Records would be liable for punishment. By 1438, thanks to the development of the various astronomical instruments discussed above, along with other advances in time measurement, solar and lunar eclipses could be forecast with such accuracy that the ceremonies were held without any errors.

The dedicated efforts of Sejong and his scholars to further the study of astronomy bore fruit in 1442 with the publication of *Chiljongsan (*A Calculation of the Motions of the Seven Celestial Determinants; the Sun and Moon, Mercury, Mars, Jupiter, Venus and Saturn). in two volumes, ten years after Sejong had first directed Chong Cho and Chong In-ji to design the *Kanui* which enabled Choson to compile its own almanac.

The first volume of the *Calculation* was a revision of the existing Yuan and Ming Dynasty almanacs, the *Susiryok* and the *Ta-tungryok*, with the primary point of reference changed to Seoul. Now, Korean scientists were able to calculate the position of all the planets with respect to the Korean capital, as well as the times and occurrences of solar and lunar eclipses. The book calculates one year to be 365.2425 days, and one month to be 29.530593 days, values correct to six significant figures compared to today's calculations.

The key feature of the second volume of the *Calculation of the Motions of the Seven Celestial Determinants* was that it used new, recalculated standards of measurement. Up to this time, the Chinese tradition had been followed, assigning 365.25 degrees to a circumference, 100 minutes to one degree, and 100 seconds to one minute. For the publication of *Calculation*, these standards were revised so that a circumference consisted of 360 degrees, 1 degree of 60 minutes, and 1 minute of 60 seconds, corresponding to the standards universally used today.

A Calculation of the Motions of the Seven Celestial Determinants is regarded as one of the most impressive astronomical achievements of its day. In 1442, when it was published, the only civilized nations capable of producing astronomical calculations to such a high degree of accuracy were China and Arabia. Two hundred forty years later, the book would be introduced to Japan by Royal ambassador Pak In-gi, thus enabling Japan to publish a native almanac compiled with respect to its own position.

9. Scientific Progress in 15th Century Korea

A great number of noteworthy scientific achievements were made in the Korean peninsula during the opening years of the 15th century. The advances made in the disciplines of astronomy, meteorology, and printing are among the most ingenious and impressive in world history, and deserve recognition alongside the other distinguished accomplishments of the Far East. They could be seen as a bridge between the era of Islamic scientific progress in the middle ages and the supremacy of Western science in modern times. As mentioned in the introduction, the Japanese Dictionary of Science and Technography (科學史奇術史事典), published in 1983, recorded that of the major scientific achievements of the period 1400-1450, 29 were made in Korea, 5 in China, and 26 in the rest of the world. This calls into question the commonly-held view that science and technology owe their conception and development largely to Western pioneers in the late second millennium.

This chapter explores the driving forces behind scientific progress in 15th century Korea, and examines in details the initiatives of King Sejong in the field of technology.

Spirit of Innovation

The ambitious vision pursued by the sovereigns of the early Choson dynasty in relation to the study and development of science will not seem unremarkable to anyone familiar with this period of oriental history. The attempt of Sejong and his father Taejong to raise the standard of printing by means of the new metal type is an obvious example of this visionary spirit. After his coronation, Taejong announced to his courtiers, "When governing a state, one must awaken to virtue and the principles of wisdom through wide reading, so as to achieve the state of one who, in the words of Confucius, 'Becomes a good master of himself, then of his household, then of his nation, and finally, of all that lies beneath the Heavens.' Since we are across the sea from China, Chinese books rarely enter our kingdom. Moreover, since wooden printing blocks break easily and are difficult to make in the first place, it would be a hard task to print all the books of the world. Therefore, we will make letters in metal type, and if we print and distribute every book that falls into our hands, great benefits will follow."

Taejong's ministers approved of the principles behind King Taejong's vision, but as countless obstacles would naturally obstruct the path of so ambitious a project, they initially opposed it, asserting that the task of casting the type would be too difficult to achieve. But Taejong never abandoned his conviction, and after months of trial and error, finally succeeded in creating several hundred thousand letters of bronze type, called the *Kyemi* font, in 1403. Although it has often been described as little more than an improvement on the movable metal type invented in the 13th century, the difficulties encountered in its manufacture were such that it would be more appropriate to regard it as a reinvention of the original type.

During the casting of the *Kabin* font (1434), Sejong encouraged Yi Chon, chief superintendent of the printing office by reminding him of this former achievement. "When Taejong established a foundry to cast metal type, everyone in the Royal Court voiced their opposition to the project in view of the difficulties involved. But Taejong did not abandon his determination and proceeded with his plans."

Whenever the resolve of the court scientists wavered because of setbacks in their research, the vigorous encouragement from the two kings gave them the strength to reawaken their determination and rise above their negative preconceptions and perceived limitations. This pioneering spirit, which sought constantly to build the possible out of the impossible, was the force behind achievements such as the 365-volume medical encyclopedia, the dissemination of advanced farming techniques which enabled continuous cultivation of the land for the first time in the history of Korea, and the compilation of Korea's own astronomical almanac.

A New Approach to the Selection of Officials

The society of 15th century Korea was strictly hierarchical. Positions in government were open only to the nobility, or *yangban* class. 'Yang' means 'two' or 'both' and 'ban' means seat, position, or status. In the royal court, officials were seated to the right and left hand of the king, and this is how their name was derived. *Yangban* families married into one another and lived apart from the other classes. In the capital of Hanyang – present day Seoul – their houses were in the Northern and Southern districts. Generally speaking, only members of this hereditary rank were eligible to enter for the state examinations, which were the sole gateway to government office.

In Choson Korea, there were three types of state examination: Literary, Military and Technical. Since proficiency in literary studies was more highly regarded than expertise in more practical studies such as law, medicine and foreign languages, the highest roles in government were awarded to those who had been successful in the literary examinations. But the literary state examinations were limited to the offspring of a legal wife of *yangban* class; and the children of a *yangban*'s concubine could only enter for the science-based technical examinations, and so such men generally went on to become professionals such as physicians, inspectors, auditors, translators and technicians.

The Class System of Choson Korea

Yangban ("The Right and Left")
Scholars and Military Commanders

Chung-in ("The Middle Men")
Physicians, Inspectors, Auditors, Translators, Technicians and others

Sang-in ("The Commoners")
The greater populace, consisting mainly of farmers

Coun-in ("The Lesser Commoners")
Private and public servants, professional entertainers, jesters, butchers, shamans and others

Those born to the concubines of *yangban* households usually lived in the middle district of the capital, and were thus called *chung-in*, or 'middle men'. While still considered in a broad sense to be part of the ruling class, the *chung-in* were in fact treated very differently. In Choson society, those who worked in science and technology tended to be of *chung-in* rank, and were invariably victims of discrimination and repression when selection was being made for government office. In the early 15th century, however, a large number of talented scientists were chosen for important offices by King Sejong, since he believed that ability and talent were more important than social status. The promoted *chung-in* received such favorable treatment, in fact, that they found themselves drawing the envy of certain literary officials.

In his *Collected Works of History*, Yi Keung-ik records that from time to time King Sejong would visit the Chomsong Observatory to have discussions with the astronomers, and have good wine brought to them when their talk was over. He promoted the scientists Yun Sa-ong, Yi Mu-rim, Choi Chon-gu, and Chong Yong-guk to the governorship of the districts surrounding Seoul, saying, "Since I have witnessed the hard work and effort of the officers of astronomy this day, I now bestow on them positions of responsibility in government, and I believe my intention to be neither futile nor unwise." After this, the Royal Secretariat is said to have petitioned the king twice daily for several days: "Your Highness, there is no one who is not shocked by the prospect of several important provinces falling under the governance of a vulgar rabble such as these men are. We beseech Your Highness to withdraw your decree with all haste." Sejong, however, refused to change his orders, and continued to praise the work and efforts of the astronomers.

The most notable example of Sejong's resolution to promote talent regardless of social status is his decision in the case of Chang Yong-sil. This decision turned out to be a very prudent one. Chang, who later became famous for his invention of the sundial and automated water-clock, began his career as a servant in the government offices at Tongrae. According to the *Sejong Sillok*, his father was from Sohangju in China, and his mother was a *kisaeng* (professional entertainer) from Tongrae. Despite his lowly origin, he displayed an exceptional talent for mechanics and engineering. When he learned of Chang's gifts, Sejong sent him to China so that he could familiarize himself with the most advanced theories in technology and science. After studying at various observatories in China, Chang was relieved of his servant status and appointed a Royal Scientist in the seventh year of Sejong's reign (1425). When the decision for his appointment to office was first made known, opposition from several ministers temporary halted proceedings altogether. When Taejong later added his support to Chang's case at the next discussion of his appointment, he was finally given the undisputed right to become an official of the Royal Household.

Having been raised from servant status to the rank of Royal Scientist within a single day, Chang continued to enjoy the favor of Sejong for the twenty years that followed. He went on to contribute to the design and construction of the celestial globe, the astrolabe, the sundial, automatic water clock and the rain gauge, certain of which were solely the result of his own work. He also worked with Yi Chon to improve printing technology, and so made great a many contributions to the study of science before he died.

Systematic and Collaborative Research

Scientific studies undertaken in early Choson Korea were distinguished by the use of nationwide workforces, who were coordinated in separate teams to drive and support important research projects. In the project to produce *A Plain Guide to Farming*, for example, Sejong directed that regional governors in the southernmost provinces should see that all experienced farmers were interviewed and that the details of their expertise be sent in report form to the Jade Hall, so that the techniques appropriate to the various climates of each part of the country could be understood and categorized appropriately. The Jade Hall scholars, in turn, were ordered to research all the available literature on farming, and to review the vast collection of information that had recently been sent to them in order to consolidate all the research into a single book, to be printed with wooden blocks for distribution to farmers throughout the country. No scholar today could hope to conduct research on a similar scale. A research system of this kind utilized the resources of an entire nation, and was only possible thanks to the monarchic system of government which existed in Korea at that time.

When the largest astronomical instruments and observatory in the country's history were under construction, a special committee was set up to support collaborative research among the participators in the project. When Yun Sa-ong, Choi Chon-gu and Chang Yong-sil returned from study leave in Ming China, Sejong established a Department for the Design of Astronomical Instruments, assigning to it the responsibility for the new project. After the first model proved successful in its testing phases, Sejong eagerly embarked upon the construction of a large-scale observatory.

Chungbo Munhon Pigo (A History of the Civilization of Korea) (1908) records that "Chong Cho, Chong In-ji and others searched the classical texts, while Yi Chon, Chang Yong-sil and others participated in the construction work." This description, though brief, demonstrates the typical division of labour between theoretical research and practical management within one team.

These astronomical projects were all carried out with a view to the eventual composition of an independent almanac. To achieve this end, a team of researchers was formed by Royal order to undertake the necessary mathematical calculations for the almanac, and the publication of the final version. Yi Sun-ji, Kim Tam and Chong Hum-ji were the main scientists who worked on this task.

It is unclear how many people were involved in the publication of *A Classified Collection of Medical Prescriptions*, the medical encyclopedia. Kim Ye-mong, Yu Song-won, and Min Po-hwa were in charge of collecting and categorizing the basic material for the first phase of this project. Kim Min, Sin Sok-jo, Yi Ye and Kim Su-on worked as the main researchers, while the medical officers Kim Sun-ui, Choi Yun, Kim You-ji and others took a key role in compiling and editing the research material. Grand Prince Yi Sa-chol, Yi Sa-sun, the Grand Prince Anpyong, and others, also participated as supervisors of the project, with Roh Chung-rae as the overall head of research. The resulting work, which numbered over 365 books, was therefore the result of the combined efforts of a great number of people, although only the 14 scholars and medical officers, as the key contributors, were mentioned in the official records.

The Introduction of Foreign Technology

Sejong wanted to bring world-class technology into Korea, but he was also keen to ensure that it was properly adapted for domestic use. Sejong was not an unquestioning admirer of China, but nor was he naturally prejudiced against other nations. As King, he endeavored to learn everything that he thought would be helpful for the development of science in his country, even from Japan, which was at that time considered as an underdeveloped nation in Asia.

When research was being carried out for the *Collection of Native Korean Prescriptions*, Sejong sent experts abroad to collect information on various medical ingredients, in order to compare Korean medicine with that of other countries. When engaged in the design and construction of observational equipment, similarly, he dispatched the scientists Chang, Yun, Choi, and others to China, so that they could remain familiar with the latest developments in astronomy. The regular envoys that Sejong sent to China to acquire knowledge in the various spheres of scientific study were ordered to bring back as many texts and treatises as they could.

Improvements in naval technology often occurred through comparison with Japanese vessels. This was partly due to a desire to counter the attacks of Japanese pirates, who since the period of the Three Kingdoms had ceaselessly plundered and looted Korea's coastal regions. The naval craftsmen of Korea therefore went to great lengths to build ships that were superior to the Japanese pirate vessels, and even invited Japanese technicians to learn from them. They compared their naval craft with those of other nations as well, and did not hesitate to learn from their points of superiority.

The rapid advances made in science and technology, which were achieved by a combination of good fortune and effort, significantly improved the living standards of the Korean people. It was with this end in mind that Sejong sought out the most talented scientists, supported them, and encouraged them to perform to the best of their ability, in the belief that they would determine the success or failure of his policy to bring practical benefit to the people of his country.

King Sejong should not be thought of as a mere champion of scientific progress. The greatest of all scientific achievements in 15th century Korea was surely the creation of *Hangul*, the Korean alphabet. However much knowledge we can acquire, it is of little use without a medium which enables us to share it with others. Created in the awareness that knowledge is power, and as a means of making knowledge available to all people to enable them to better themselves, *Hangul* is a consummate work of scientific achievement. Sejong, who must have struggled for many days to produce this simple but ingenious method of writing, was in this sense a true scientist, who loved and sought after truth, and endeavored all his life to share its fruits with others.

VI. Invention of the Korean Alphabet

1. *Hunmin Chongum*, The Proper Sounds for Instructing the People

> The spoken language of our country is different from that of China and does not suit the Chinese characters. Therefore amongst uneducated people there have been many who, having something that they wish to put into words, have been unable to express their feelings in writing. I am greatly distressed because of this, and so I have made twenty eight new letters. Let everyone practice them at their ease, and adapt them to their daily use.
>
> –King Sejong's *Preface to Hunmin Chongum*

Widely considered as the greatest legacy of King Sejong the Great, the Korean alphabet or Hangul was created in 1443, the 25th year of Sejong's reign. Three years later in 1446, it was set out in published form together with a manual explaining it in detail. Sejong named the alphabet and its accompanying volume *Hunmin Chongum* (The Proper Sounds for Instructing the People). The Korean alphabet is nowadays commonly referred to as Hangul, which means 'the Script of Han (Korea)' or 'the Great Script'.

Of the six thousand languages in existence, only one hundred have their own alphabets. Of these one hundred languages, Hangul is the only alphabet made by an individual for which the theory and motives behind its creation have been fully set out and explained. Roman characters have their origins in the hieroglyphics of Egypt and the syllabic Phoenician alphabets, and had to undergo a process of gradual evolution to become what they are today. Chinese characters, similarly, began as inscriptions on bones and tortoise shells, and took thousands of years to reach their current form.

Hangul is neither based on ancient written languages nor an imitation of another set of characters, but an alphabet unique to Korea. *Hunmin Chongum*, which contained a systematic analysis of the new alphabet, is also without precedent in history, and September 10th, its original date of publication, has been designated 'Hangul Day' by the Korean Government in recognition of its importance. UNESCO has also created an award called the 'King Sejong Literacy Prize', as part of its worldwide campaign against illiteracy.

Hunmin Chongum is only 33 pages long, consisting of four introductory pages written by King Sejong, and twenty-nine pages of commentary added by Jade Hall scholars. Its structure is orderly and its content logical and scientific. The original version, for 500 years thought to have been lost, was rediscovered in a deserted house near Andong in 1940. It is currently being kept in the Kansong Museum as National Treasure no. 70, and was included in UNESCO's World Cultural Heritage in 1997.

2. The Principles and Theory behind Hangul

China was the superpower of 15th century Asia, and its culture, outlook, and written language had a considerable presence and influence in Korean society. Since the tongues of the two nations belonged to different linguistic families, however, Korean was not ideally suited to be expressed in Chinese letters. In Chinese, sentences are qualified with particles, whereas in Korean inflections and suffixes are used to add or modify meaning.

As both a scholar and a cultural pioneer, Sejong was able to analyze the basic units of medieval Korean speech using his own knowledge of linguistics, and finally succeeded in alphabetizing it in the *Hunmin Chongum*. An entry in the *Sejong Sillok* on 30 December, the 25th year of the King's reign, shows that the *Hunmin Chongum* was Sejong's own invention: "This month the King has personally created 28 letters of *Onmun* (the vernacular script)... Though simple and concise, it is capable of infinite variations and is called *Hunmin Chongum*."

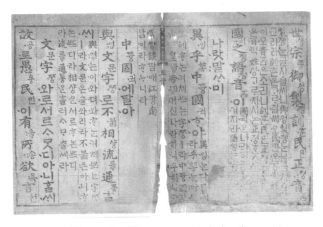

Hunmin Chongum (original copy)

According to the *Explanations and Examples of the Hunmin Chongum*, the basic consonant symbols were schematic drawings of the human speech organs as they articulate certain sounds, while the other consonants were formed by adding strokes to these five basic shapes.

The velar ㄱ (k) depicts the root of the tongue blocking the throat.

The alveolar ㄴ(n) depicts the outline of the tongue touching the upper palate.

The labial ㅁ (m) depicts the outline of the mouth.

The dental ㅅ (s) depicts the outline of the incisor.

The laryngeal ㅇ (zero initial) depicts the outline of the throat.

The pronunciation of the aspirated velar ㅋ (k') is more forceful than that of ㄱ (k), and therefore a stoke is added.

The vowel symbols were formed after the three fundamental symbols of Eastern philosophy.

The round · represents Heaven.

The flat ㅡ represents Earth,

The upright ㅣ represents Man.

These three basic shapes are combined to derive other vowels: ㅏ, ㅑ, ㅓ, ㅕ, ㅗ. ㅛ. ㅜ, ㅠ. The consonants and vowels each represent a phoneme, or unit of speech, and together the letters make a syllable. For example, 'Moon' in Korean is "달", which consists of: ㄷ(consonant)+ ㅏ (vowel)+ㄹ(consonant). In other words, Korean is both an alphabetic and a syllabic language.

Founded on philosophical as well as scientific principles, *Hangul* embodies certain elements of the Confucian outlook: in traditional Eastern thought, *yin* stands for the concepts of feminine, passive, dark, dry and cold, while the *yang* encompasses the masculine, active, bright, humid and hot. From the interaction between these two principles arise the five elements of Wood, Fire, Earth, Metal and Water, which represent dynamic processes rather than physical entities.

Corresponding to the principle of *yin-yang* and the five elements, each vowel and consonant in *Hangul* is assigned the properties of either *yin* or *yang*, and the five basic consonants represent the five elements, according to their place of articulation.

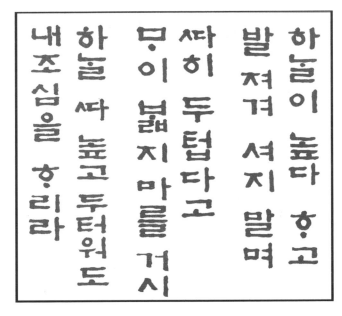

Hangul Calligraphy

3. Difficulties with the Introduction of *Hangul*

In addition to the heavy burden of serving a nation and its people, the passing of time left King Sejong suffering from neuralgia, diabetes, and poor eyesight. The King devoted all his remaining powers to the creation of *Hangul*. Even when visiting the hot springs of Onyang and Chongju for medical treatment, he took with him his books on linguistics and continued his writing and research. Finally, in the winter of 1443, the most significant development in Korea's five thousand year history was finally completed.

From the moment of its conception, however, *Hangul* encountered strong opposition and censure from the King's court. Choi Manli, a senior scholar of the Jade Hall, presented the following petition to the King, fiercely criticizing the new alphabet:

"Since the new alphabet is so easily understood, I fear that the people will fall into laziness and never make efforts to learn. Those who do not use Chinese characters but other letters and alphabets, such as the Mongols, Sohans, Jurchens, Japanese and Tibetans, are all barbarians without exception. To use new letters would surely make us barbarians ourselves."

He continued, "Why does Your Highness seek to alter a language that has been used since early antiquity and has no ill effects, and place alongside it a set of coarse and vulgar characters of no worth at all? Is not this script, moreover, a mere transcription of the words spoken by the peasants, without the slightest resemblance to the original Chinese characters? The new alphabet is in truth no more than an eccentric and ill-considered crudity, an obstruction to literary progress, and of no possible benefit to government. I maintain, Your Highness, that we will find no virtue in the script, however long we deliberate upon the matter."

A call for universal literacy was in King Sejong's day something of an anachronism. It would have been considered by many unnecessary and undesirable for the general population to be able to read. Some of those in power would even have considered it dangerous to put a tool as politically important as writing in the hands of the common people. The creation of a new alphabet was further regarded as a challenge and affront to the long tradition and authority of the use of Chinese script and to the Sino-centric world order. Sejong was well aware of the gulf that existed between his ideal and its realisation. Thus, rather than attacking the arguments of his opponents directly, he expressed his beliefs with moderation and firmness:

"Sol Chong of Silla created *Yidu* [a method of transcribing the Korean language based on sound and meaning of the Chinese characters] for the people, and now I too have made a new alphabet for them. Why do you agree that Sol Chong was in the right while maintaining that your King is in the wrong? If I do not tend to the nation's language, who else will? I myself take great delight in classical literature. Therefore it cannot be said that I am doing this simply because I prefer what is new to what is old".

Sejong resolutely pursued his policy of promulgating the new alphabet, and shortly afterwards several literary works were created in new Korean script. Chief among these are the *Yongbi Ochonga* (Songs of Flying Dragons), a eulogy of the virtues of the royal ancestors, *Sokpo Sangjol* (Episodes from the Life of the Buddha) and *Worin Chongang Chigok* (Songs of the Moon's Reflection on Thousand Rivers), a poem comparing Shakyamuni Buddha's enlightenment of all sentient beings to the moon's reflection in the rivers of the world. Sejong delivered his Royal Ordinances both in Chinese and the new Korean script, and public notices for the common people were also now written in *Hangul*. The new alphabet also

Promulgation of *Hangul* in 1446

became a compulsory area of study in the State Examination.

Neither the ingenuity behind *Hangul* nor the strenuous efforts of the King, however, were able to alter centuries of habit and custom overnight. Korean civil servants and scholars would continue to use the revered Chinese characters in official and unofficial documents for the next four hundred years.

4. An Alphabet for the 21st Century

The true worth of Sejong's *Hangul* has been proven in the course of time, and now draws interest and admiration from linguistic scholars around the world. *Hangul* has now replaced Chinese characters in all Korean books and newspapers, and the great invention of King Sejong has, after five centuries, finally achieved its goal.

The Korean alphabet is like no other writing system in the world. It is the only alphabet completely native to East Asia…The structure of the Korean alphabet shows a sophisticated understanding of phonological science that was not equaled in the West until modern times. –Robert Ramsey, "The Korean Alphabet", *King Sejong the Great*, p. 198

We may well marvel at the outstanding simplicity and convenience of Hangul. Whether or not it is ultimately the best of all conceivable scripts for Korean, Hangul must unquestionably rank as one of the great intellectual achievements of humankind. –Geoffrey Sampson, *Writing Systems: A Linguistic Introduction*, p. 144.

One of the most unique and interesting features of the Korean alphabet is the strict correspondence it shows between graphic shape and graphic function. Not only are the shapes of the consonants of a pattern different from those of the vowels, but even within these two main groups the shapes decided upon by Sejong clarify other important relationships… No other alphabet in the world is so beautifully, and sensibly, rational… It is really impossible to withhold admiration for this conception of a shape-function relationship and for the way it was carried out. There is nothing like it in all the long and varied history of writing. It would be quite enough merely to have the systematic shapes within classes. But for those shapes themselves to be rationalized on the basis of the speech organs associated with their sounds—that is unparalleled grammatological luxury! The Korean phonologists were skillful indeed, but they were not lacking in creative imagination either.

–G.K. Ledyard. "The Korean Language Reform of 1446: The Origin, Background, and Early History of the Korean Alphabet", p. 199-203.

The king's 28 letters have been described by scholars as "the world's best alphabet" and "the most scientific system of writing." They are an ultra-rational system devised from scratch to incorporate three unique features. First, Hangul vowels can be distinguished at a glance from Hangul consonants… Even more remarkable, the shape of each consonant depicts the position in which the lips, mouth, or tongue is held to pronounce that letter…Twentieth-century scholars were incredulous that those resemblances could really be intentional until 1940, when they discovered the original draft of King Sejong's 1446 proclamation and found the logic explicitly spelled out.

–Jared Diamond, "Writing Right", *Discovery*, June 1994

In the Age of Information, Hangul keeps its competitive edge over other alphabets. On a computer keyboard, the consonants are arranged on the left, the vowels on the right, and words formed as consonants and vowels are typed alternately. In terms of ergonomics, this allows for maximization of productivity by, *inter alia*, an efficient distribution of tiredness in the fingers. Moreover, the fact that each letter has one single sound is extremely advantageous…Since the Chinese is unable to be accommodated on the keyboard, its input is through Roman characters, and the speed of information management similarly suffers in case of Japanese, as it relies heavily on the Chinese letters. With Hangul, as the sound changes, the frequency also changes at a fixed rate, allowing speech recognition by computers to be done logically and easily. The sound and the writing of Hangul, therefore, have a vast sphere of application, from the system of translation to the internet. –Yi Hwa-yong, *Humanism, the Power of Korean Culture,* p18-19.

The perfect alphabet may be a hopelessly remote ideal, but it is possible to do a better job than history has made of the western alphabet, in any of its manifestations. We know this because there is an alphabet that is about as far along the road towards perfection as any alphabet is likely to get. Emerging in Korea in mid-fifteenth century, it has the status among language scholars normally reserved for classic works of art. In its simplicity, efficiency and elegance, this alphabet is alphabet's epitome, a star among alphabets, a national treasure for Koreans and 'one of the great intellectual achievements of humankind', in the judgment of British linguist, Geoffrey Sampson.
    –John Man, *Alpha Beta: how 26 letters shaped the Western world*

Linguists of many nations acknowledge the originality and philosophy behind *Hangul,* and its logical and pragmatic basis. More valuable than the alphabet itself, however, is the spirit of King Sejong embodied within it. His sincere wish that all the people of his country should learn to express their thoughts at will is the true pride of Korea and a spiritual heritage to be shared with the world. Used now as an alternative alphabet for minority peoples who have no written language, it continues even today to be a lamp illuminating illiteracy and ignorance.

VII. Concluding Words

A tree deep-rooted, unshaken in the wind,

Its blossoms fair and its fruits abundant.

A spring deep-founded, unceasing in the drought,

Its stream flowing down to the open sea.

- Song of Flying Dragons, Canto 2

Unlike many other kings given the title 'Great' by posterity, Sejong's greatness did not lie in brute force or in the conquering and subduing of other peoples, but in a series of intellectual and cultural achievements that have continued to benefit his nation through many generations, and which enrich the lives of his people today.

Through his intelligence, creative energy, compassion, and good judgment, the King worked with untiring dedication to free his countrymen from poverty, injustice, and ignorance. He surrounded himself with capable scholars and scientists, whose ingenuity found an ordered and splendid means of expression under his leadership.

It is for this reason that the name of Sejong is given to many streets, schools, research institutes, cultural centers, and even businesses in modern Korea. Over time, he has come also to win the respect and admiration of people outside Korea as well. The American linguist Dr. Macaulay has been celebrating Hangul Day for the past 30 years. On September 9 of every year, he prepares Korean food and invites his colleagues, students, and close friends to celebrate the creation of the

Korean alphabet. Japanese scientist Watanabe Gatso of the International Astronomical Union chose to give a minor planet he discovered the name of '7365 Sejong 1996 QV'. And in Warsaw, Poland, one of the leading high schools has recently changed its name to Sejong High School and added the Korean language to its curriculum.

Sejong was a king who served the people with reverence and humility, who promoted the power and beauty of culture out of love and benevolence, and instilled in his country a sense of independence and a new cultural identity. He possessed a deep respect for history and tradition, valued learning and scholarship, and led his country forward with bold and innovative reforms. Dressed in patched clothing and living beneath a humble roof, he never faltered in his sense of duty and responsibility even in the days when his work on the alphabet caused him to become blind. He was a father to the poor, the weak, the ignorant and even those who sinned.

Sejong, the fourth and greatest monarch of Choson Korea, continued after his death to be a deep root and inexhaustible spring for all Korean people. And despite the many words that have been written about this king, and may yet be written, his virtues can never be described in full.

Royal Tomb of King Sejong

Appendix

The Sillok: the Royal Annals of Choson Dynasty

A great deal of our knowledge about the reign of King Sejong comes from the pages of the *Sillok*, or Annals of the Choson Dynasty. Covering four hundred and seventy two years of history (1392-1863), they record the acts of twenty five kings, beginning with the founder of the dynasty, King Taejo, and ending with King Choljong. The total work consists of some 1,893 books, of which 163 make up the *Sejong Sillok*, which records the acts of King Sejong. It is therefore one of the most detailed and extensive accounts of a king's reign contained in the work. A unique feature of the *Sejong Sillok* is the long postscript (Vol. 128-163), not found in the records of the other kings. It contains diagrams, maps, charts, musical scores, and various technical treatises on the subjects of astronomy, geography, music, and sacred and secular rites. The diverse cultural achievements of Sejong could not be adequately conveyed in chronological form, and so this second section was added with his achievements arranged thematically.

The court historians took a shorthand record of every word spoken by the king in the record called the *Sacho*, including conversations with courtiers, details of meetings, councils and other discussions of national issues, and even the king's behavior and appearance. They would follow the king everywhere in order to keep an accurate record of what he said and did. One day, King Taejong fell from his horse while out hunting, and said to his companions in embarrassment, "Do not let the historian find out about this." To his disappointment, even these words were carefully recorded in the *Sacho* by the court historian.

The knowledge that their words and deeds would remain for future generations to judge and learn from instilled a chastening fear in the rulers of Korea and prevented them from becoming tyrannical. When a king died, his successor would appoint historians from the *Chunchugwan* (Department of History) to compile an official history of the former king's reign, based on the *Sacho* and the daily chronicles and reports from the other main departments. When these annals had been completed, the document was sent to the printer, and four copies were made in order to ensure its future preservation. One of these copies was deposited at the Royal Archive in Seoul, and the other three at the cities of Songju, Chungju and Chonju, which lay in diverse parts of the kingdom. Even if one of the archives was lost because of fire or a natural disaster, the *Silloks* at the other repositories would enable it to be replaced. But during the Seven Year War (1592-1598), the entire country was engulfed in conflict and the four copies were all at risk of being destroyed. Fortunately, the copy kept at Chonju was moved to Mt. Naejang prior to a Japanese raid on that city, and thus two hundred years of history, including the reign of Sejong, were saved from being lost forever. The government used the surviving copy to replace the lost versions of the *Sillok* after the war ended, and arranged for them to be guarded in remote locations on islands and mountains, with the exception of a single copy, which was always kept in the Royal Archives.

Objectivity was considered very important in the writings that comprised the *Sillok*, since the purpose of the record was to pass on the lessons of history to subsequent generations. A clear, unbiased account of what had actually happened was therefore vital, and to ensure that this was the case, only commissioned historians were granted access to the *Sacho* and the *Sillok*. Not even the king was exempt from this rule. When Sejong expressed a wish to read the *Taejong Sillok*, in order to discover how historians had evaluated the events of his father's reign, his request was resolutely blocked by the Royal courtiers.

> The King said,
> "Now that the *Taejong Sillok* has been completed, I wish to read it for myself. What is your opinion?"
> To this the Vice-Prime Minister Maeng Sa-song replied,
> "If Your Majesty reads the *Sillok* now, future kings will wish to do the same. And if the king who reads the *Sillok* is displeased by what he sees, he will try to make changes to it, and so the royal historians will not be able to record history in its wholeness, fearing the King's punishment. In that case, Your Majesty, how can the truth be preserved for future generations?"
> The King replied, "What you say is true."
> –*Sillok*, 20 March, 13th year of Sejong's reign

Thus, neither King nor his Ministers were permitted to read the *Sillok*. For purposes of administering the state, however, it was permitted to refer to it in order to find historical precedents for an action under consideration. Even in such cases, the officer dispatched to the Royal Archive would be permitted only to copy the entries relevant to the issue in question. When new records were being placed in the archives, or when the chambers were being cleaned or ventilated, historians from Department of History were required to be present to ensure that no damage or loss occurred. The strictness of the provisions concerning the guarding and maintenance of the *Sillok* is easy to understand, considering that they contained a truthful account of both honorable and dishonorable episodes from the politics of the day, as well as discussions and critiques of the King's character and his Ministers.

The *Sillok* is a source of information on a wide range of historical and cultural aspects of the Choson Dynasty, including politics, diplomacy, military affairs, law, economics, industry, transportation, communications, social systems, customs, etiquette, art and crafts, philosophy, and religion. It provides colorful insight into the lives of people on every level of society, from the aristocracy to the common farmer, and is a rare and valuable resource for historians studying the period today.

Originally written in Chinese characters, the *Sillok* remained inaccessible to many even after it was made public. A concerted effort began in 1968 to translate the *Sillok* into Korean. Twenty five years later, 413 volumes of the translated *Sillok* had been published, and were released in CD-ROM format owing to their enormous size. From 2005 onwards, both the translation and original have been available on the internet at www.sillok.history.go.kr.

The *Sillok* is designated the 151st National Treasure of Korea, and is also listed in the register of UNESCO's 'Memory of the World' Programme (1977).

The History of the Rain Gauge

No model of *Chugugi*, the world's first rain gauge, has survived from its earliest days of existence and use under King Sejong. Today, we possess only a small number of *Chugugi*, made shortly after the 18th century. The lack of surviving early models is one of the main reasons for the current confusion surrounding the *Chugugi*'s country of origin.

In 1910, Japanese scholar Wakada Yuchi (和田雄治 1859~1918) became aware of the historical importance of the *Chugugi*, and published the photograph of the best surviving model he could find, in a dissertation. At the

time, he was a head of a meteorological station in Chemulpo. His paper was entitled "The Rain Gauge of 15th century Korea" and was sent to a number of academic acquaintances in France.

Originally a graduate in Physics from Tokyo University, Wakada Yuchi had studied Meteorology in France from 1889 to 1891. He therefore chose to write his paper in French, and submitted it to friends and scholars in the country where he had studied. It was in this way that the *Chugugi* came to be known in Europe.

The paper was first published in the January issue of the scientific journal *Nature* in 1911, and an English translation was published in the

37th issue of the *Quarterly Journal of the Royal Meteorological Society* of Britain in the same year. The *Chugugi* had now finally been made known to the world, but the photograph used in the paper was of a model made in 1770. Still the most widely used picture of the *Chugugi* in publications today, it bore the inscription "*Konryung Kyongin Owoljo*".

Seeing this inscription, Chinese scholars naturally assumed that the device had been made in China, and had found its way to Korea at a later date. '*Konryung*' was the word used in the Chinese dating system to denote the period of the Ching dynasty. '*Kyungin Owoljo*' signified that it had been made in the 5th month of the year *Kyongin* (1770). Being unaware of the fact that Koreans used Chinese terms for their dating system, they came to the conclusion that the device was of Chinese origin. As a result, Chinese textbooks present the *Chugugi* as an invention of their own homeland, and its photograph is found proudly displayed in many Chinese scientific and meteorological publications.

Neither the term *Chugugi*, however, nor any information relating to the rain-gauge, can be found anywhere in surviving Chinese literature. Nevertheless, in his great work, *Science and Civilisation in China*, the renowned scholar of Chinese scientific history Joseph Needham (1900-1995) wrote "…the rain gauge was not a Korean invention, but goes back a good deal earlier in China". In evidence of this, he cited *Suso Kujang* (數書九章), a mathematic text from the Chinese Sung Dynasty, in which the phrase "*Chugu*" was used. However, "*Chugu*", which means 'measuring precipitation' (–*gi* adding the meaning of 'device'), was not written in specific reference to the rain-gauge. Clear references to the device do appear in the *Sejong Sillok* (18 August, 1441; 8 May, 1442), and although the *Chugugi* has come to be thought of as a discovery of China, there seems little doubt that it was originally a Korean invention.

Bibliography

Bae Kichan, *Korea: Standing at a Turning Point of its History*, Wisdom House, 2005.

Geoffrey Sampson, *Writing Systems: A Linguistic Introduction*, Tuttle Publishing, 1990.

G.K. Ledyard. "The Korean Language Reform of 1446: The Origin, Background, and Early History of the Korean Alphabet" Dissertation, University of California, Berkeley, 1966.

Jared Diamond, "Writing Right", *Discovery*, June 1994.

Jeon Sang-woon, *Science under King Sejong*, King Sejong Memorial Society, 1986.

John Man, *Alpha Beta*, Headline Book Publishing Ltd., 2001.

Kim Ho, *Scientist of Choson Korea*, Humanist, 2003.

Pak Pyong-ho, *Legal Systems under King Sejong*, King Sejong Memorial Society, 1986.

Pak Song-rae, *How the Chugugi had become the Chinese Invention*, History for Tomorrow, Vol. 18, 2004.

The Academy of Korean Studies, *Culture under King Sejong*, Taehak Publications, 2002.

Yi Hwa-hyong, *Humanism: The Power of Korean Culture*, Kookhak, 2004.

Yi Song-mu, *What is Choson Royal Sillok?*, Tongbang Media, 2002.

Young-key Kim-Renaud, *King Sejong the Great*, Singu Munhwa Publications, 1998.

Published by Diamond Sutra Recitation Group

Please direct all inquries to kingsejong@mail.com

New York
158-16 46th Ave.
Flushing, NY 11358
▪ 718-539-9108

Atlanta
4619 Chattahoochee Crossing
Marietta, GA 30067
▪ 678-978-2331

New Jersey
190 Mountain Rd
Ringoes, NJ 08551
▪ 609-3339422

Germany
Hiltistr, 7a 86916
Kaufering, Germany
▪ 49-8191-70618

Los Angeles
2197 Seaview Dr
Fullenton, CA 92833
▪ 562-644-8949

England
57 Amberwood Rise
New Malden, Surrey
KT3 5JQ
▪ 44-208-942-1640

Diamond Sutra Recitation Group is a non-profit organization
dedicated to the cultivation of the mind